TO: JOSLU.

2nd AERi HG

Disrupting LinkedIn:

The Definitive Guide to Generating Leads,

Receiving Referrals and Attracting High-End

Clients Through Marketing on LinkedIn

By: Yakov Savitskiy

Proud to be a Pi!

- *[signature]*

Disrupting LinkedIn:
The Definitive Guide to Generating Leads, Receiving
Referrals and Attracting High-End Clients Through
Marketing on LinkedIn

All Rights Reserved

COPYRIGHT © 2017 Yakov Savitskiy

ISBN-13: 978-1973994619
ISBN-10: 1973994615

Cover design by Sooraj Mathew

Dedication

I'd like to dedicate this book to everyone who believed in me and continues to believe in me as a person who is operating on tremendous integrity and providing tremendous value to the market. For everyone who has trusted in me and continues to trust in me, both on personal and professional levels, this book is dedicated to you.

Table of Contents

Acknowledgments

Without the help of a great deal of people, I wouldn't have been able to produce this book, and at such a high level of quality.

I'd like to thank all my clients, from the people who I have worked with on a one-on-one basis to the people who have invested in my digital programs. I appreciate you putting your trust in me and my company when it comes to LinkedIn marketing.

I'd also like to thank my editor, Hilary Jastram, who has helped make this process nearly seamless and has been able to help me put out a book of which I am proud. Thank you also to Ryan Stewman for writing the foreword of this book and for his continued support and encouragement.

Additionally, I'd like to acknowledge Jessica Lamonde, whose satirical Facebook post gave me the idea for the title of this book and the name of the Disrupting LinkedIn community.

Lastly, I'd like to thank all the influencers and marketers who have come before me and helped to blaze the trail for the content and strategies within the pages of this book.

Foreword by Ryan Stewman

We live in a time where it's easier to connect with influencers than ever before. Social media has changed the game for small business owners all the way up to Fortune 500 companies. For business professionals, there's no better platform available than LinkedIn.

Turns out the average LinkedIn user earns $115,000 per year. The site is literally a honey hole of high-earning professionals who are the most cherry of all leads. Although LinkedIn has an unlimited pool of prospects waiting to connect and exchange business, it's not a very busy site. This makes it easy for you to get on the site, stand out and close sales from it.

Sites like Facebook, Twitter, Reddit, and Pinterest are where most people "hang out." The average user on Facebook spends 30 minutes a day scrolling their newsfeed. The average user on LinkedIn logs in for just 17 minutes per month. With LinkedIn at 500 million users and Facebook at over two billion, you can see where most people are hanging out. But if you're not looking for average people, and instead, trying to find six-figure, C-level executives, LinkedIn is your site.

For seven years, I focused on marketing my consulting business on Facebook only. I mean, I had a LI profile and all that but I never really spent any time on the site. I was truly a 17-minute-per-month man. In February 2017, Facebook kicked me off their site for 30 days. About that same time, I had the pleasure of meeting Yakov in Denver, Colorado.

I spent those 30 days marketing myself on LinkedIn using the strategies that Yakov taught me when we met up. In 30 days, I grew my network organically by over 1,500 connections as well as added another $35,000 to my monthly income.

As it turns out, the users on the site are starving for attention, connections, and information. All I had to do was follow some of the easy-to-implement strategies you'll read about in this book, and it was a snap to make connections and sales on LinkedIn. Up until the 30-day Facebook suspension, I had paid LinkedIn ZERO attention. Now, I'm on the site daily making sales.

While the idiots on Facebook argue about Donald Trump, the professionals on LinkedIn are brainstorming on how to make their next million. Which crowd would you rather spend your time with?

You're about to learn some amazing ideas from an extremely intelligent guy. I can't urge you enough to take action on what you read. Getting exposure and engagement on LinkedIn is a breeze if you follow Yakov's plan.

The fact that you're reading this book means you have an unfair advantage over everyone else who hasn't read it. Take action on the information. Start organizing your profile, connecting with influencers and following Yakov's plan. In 60 days, you'll be glad you did due to all the extra leads and sales that will come from LinkedIn.

Lastly, I want to thank the author for writing this book. His advice on LI has helped me earn a lot of money. Now, you have the opportunity to allow it to do the same or more for you. It's a matter of doing the work. Let's get started.

Ryan Stewman, CEO of Break Free Academy
Hardcorecloser.com

Introduction

When I first came onto the scene as a LinkedIn marketer, it was surprising to discover the small minority of business owners, marketers, and sales professionals who were taking advantage of such a tremendous opportunity. It became a little repetitive as I started hearing the same thing over and over again from prospective clients throughout the country. Everyone would say they'd been a LinkedIn user for a while, but that they hadn't generated much, if any business from LinkedIn. In this book, you'll discover a new way of using LinkedIn and marketing on LinkedIn. You'll find that I'll provide a wide array of tangible strategies and tactics you can apply right away. With so much misconception and misinformation about marketing on LinkedIn, I had no choice but to write this book.

Now, let me make a couple of things clear. I have absolutely no dislike or disdain for LinkedIn as a company and a social network. Quite the contrary. I am a huge fan of LinkedIn and the direction the company has been taking as of late. As you'll discover in this book, there's never been a better time to start marketing on LinkedIn. The words "Disrupting

LinkedIn" in the title really mean disrupting the old way of using and marketing on LinkedIn. My goal with this book is to give you a new set of tools which will combine the core foundations of Direct Response Marketing, and Sales, and Networking along with the amazing tools that the LinkedIn social media platform provides. That said, the contents of this book in no way, shape, or form have any direct correlation with LinkedIn as a company and are fully expressed as my individual views. I am not an employee, spokesperson, or representative of LinkedIn, nor do I claim to have any direct affiliation.

As you read this book, I encourage you to have an open mind, and more importantly, I encourage you to take action and implement the strategies I lay out for you. Without implementation, this information is useless, and you are better off spending your time on other things than reading another book on marketing.

The beginning of the book will introduce you to the concepts we'll talk about and help you understand, even more so than you do now, why there has never been a better time to market on LinkedIn. From there, I'll take you through many of the systems I personally use as well as the systems I help clients install to generate leads, receive referrals, and attract high-end clients. Of course, the disadvantage of writing a book is that there's no way to fit in all the information I can provide to you in these pages. That's why I highly encourage you to visit Linkedleads.Us to learn more about some of our digital courses as well as to learn more about applying for an opportunity to work with me directly. I look forward to being your tour guide as we journey together into exploring a new way to implement LinkedIn marketing.

Chapter One: LinkedIn Nightmares

When you read the title of this book, you probably wondered why in the world someone would write a book titled *Disrupting LinkedIn* and what purpose this sort of book could serve for you. Whether you're a business owner, you're a marketer, you're in sales, or you're just plain curious as to why I used this title, what you'll truly discover as you go through the chapters of this book is that it is about much more than just LinkedIn. It's also about much more than LinkedIn marketing or even social media technology.

You know all those terms constantly getting tossed around on a daily basis when it comes to social media marketing? You're bound to have heard them. Well, let me assure you, this book is about a lot more than buzzwords.

This book is *really* all about identifying and solving that one big headache. It's that one big nightmare that plagues so many businesses around the world today. If you're a marketer or sales professional, you can probably guess what I'm talking about. It's the huge problem everyone wants the magic solution to: how to solve the challenge of generating more opportunities and how to find ways to get in front of more qualified prospects.

The core and the lifeblood of any business is the sale. What would you need in order to make more sales? Being in front of more qualified prospects would certainly help, no matter your position or industry. This book was written to teach you how to use LinkedIn as a primary resource for getting in front of qualified prospects and getting them in a position where you can make the sale, grow your business, and enable yourself to do business with more high-end clients.

There's also a reason this chapter is called "LinkedIn Nightmares." LinkedIn offers so much untapped potential for businesses across all sorts of verticals. In a moment, we'll get into why LinkedIn is not just a B2B platform anymore and what types of B2C and even B2G opportunities there are on LinkedIn as well.

The massive challenge, the huge struggle that's plaguing so many businesses and sales professionals across the world and remains a conundrum to this day, is still this question: "How do I get in front of qualified prospects who are actually interested in buying my products or services?"

In fact, most companies and business executives typically use more than one strategy for booking consistent appointments with qualified prospects who are interested in their product or service.

First of all, there are the old-school methods. If you're reading this and have been in business for any length of time, a lot of these tactics are going to sound familiar, and you may even still be using many of them. The truth is that they do absolutely work. In fact, I'll be the first to tell you there are pros and cons to every prospecting method. Before we get into these other prospecting methods, I'd like to make a bold claim.

What we'll cover in this book will give you a brand-new way of prospecting and utilizing LinkedIn as your go-to source to get in front of the qualified prospects you're looking for, so you can book appointments with these prospects and turn those appointments into sales.

The most obvious of the old-school methods you're probably familiar with is the cold call. People talk about cold calling as this archaic method, yet so many people still do it. At its core, cold calling still does work. There's no question about that. However, my issue with cold calling, (and you'll hear more about my experience as a cold caller in the next few pages), is that it's often highly inefficient and ineffective.

You'll hear about even the best cold callers getting a two, three, and four percent conversion rate when it comes to setting sales appointments through cold calling. Look at it this way. If you have to set two appointments out of 100 cold calls to be considered a skilled cold caller, I want to invite you to think about the limited amount of time you have to cold call on a given day. You only have so many hours per day that you can be on the phone. The majority of cold calls go unanswered, and they're going to people who you are likely never to hear back from. Plus, there's also the hassle of getting past the good old gatekeeper, so you lose even more time.

If you've ever made a ton of cold calls, (and I certainly have), you'll realize when you make the cold calls, oftentimes, the assistant, admin, secretary, or even the prospect's spouse, are usually the ones who are serving as very strict gatekeepers. These gatekeepers are so tired of sales professionals, marketers, and business owners trying to sell them stuff. They usually know exactly who they'd like to let in and who they'll make sure to keep out. When making a cold call, the gatekeeper will likely give you a reason to not let you through to the decision maker.

Making a sale is already challenging enough as it is. As a business owner, marketer, or sales professional, you have zero chance of being effective if you can't even get to the decision maker. And one of the worst things that sales professionals and business owners run into is how to even talk to the decision maker. The crazy part is that if the decision maker just realized the value of your product or service, and if it was attractively presented to them, they would *want* to do business with you. Even though the gatekeeper is just doing their job, they are still preventing any chance of you reaching the decision maker.

There are plenty of instances of cold calling in the business world, and there are a lot of different techniques. Many sales "gurus" teach different methods of cold calling, yet even the best cold callers convert a very, very low percentage into appointments and clients. No matter what any "guru" says, the statistics behind cold calling are irrefutable, and prospecting through cold calling comes with a ceiling in terms of efficiency and effectiveness.

Now, let's talk about the cold email. A while ago, many sales professionals and even many business owners decided to seek refuge on the Internet when it came to prospecting. They decided they could send cold emails as a substitute for making cold calls. On the surface, and knowing what they did about email open rates and the Internet in general, that sounded like solid reasoning.

If you could find the email address, it was a way to reach the decision maker directly, so they would finally see your sales message. Before long, decision makers were receiving hundreds if not thousands of emails per day all with the aim of trying to sell them stuff. After experiencing this kind of bombardment, most decision makers and email service providers put systems in place to help weed out unwanted or unexpected emails.

It's ironic how email was once a communication platform that everyone took so seriously. Now, almost everyone is tired of receiving cold emails. We all hate them, and there are so many spammers out there, from Indian SEO companies to Nigerian princes. With our email inboxes becoming as saturated as they are, cold emailing has become an extremely ineffective and annoying prospecting method.

Another marketing ploy is people who pay for mailers. Direct mail is an interesting phenomenon, and it absolutely still works. Again, especially if you're a sales professional and you're not a business owner, or if you might have a limited budget, it can be quite costly to implement a direct mail campaign.

You would have to obtain a thorough understanding of direct mail marketing for your direct mail campaigns to hit your marketing goals. For example, you need the right marketing copy, and you'll need to know the tricks of actually getting the mail delivered and opened, so you don't wind up in the wastebasket.

When I was first starting in this business, I had a client who told me a story of his experience with direct mail. He was very sheepish when he confided in me and was embarrassed at the outcome, but maybe you can relate to his story. This business owner spent about $10,000 dollars in an attempt to penetrate a new market through direct mailers. He owned a fitness studio and had one person respond to his campaign. That's one person responding to a ten-thousand-dollar campaign! Regardless of whether or not that person signed up for membership, my client was devastated by the results of that campaign.

Maybe you've been there before, too. Maybe you've tried these old-school methods, and you've realized that it's time for a change. Maybe it's time for you to try a new way of getting in front of your qualified prospects, so you can get them interested, set appointments and grow your business.

That's exactly why I wrote this book and exactly why I want to talk about *Disrupting LinkedIn*. This is a new method of generating qualified leads, growing your business, getting referrals and working with more high-end clients through utilizing this under-used social media platform.

There are two more old-school methods that we haven't touched on yet. One is attending networking groups. Networking groups are an interesting concept. I discovered the fact they exist right before I went into business full-time. These networking groups are often local chapters of national and even international organizations.

Some of these organizations include BNI and LeTip groups. I'll be the first to say that these groups are great for building solid, real-world relationships. When you become a member, you can sit down once a week at a table with people who aren't direct competitors. You can enjoy a meal as you make new connections. These people can potentially refer business to you and vice versa. Some groups even pass around referral slips and have weekly referral quotas.

On the surface, the idea of networking groups is great, and there are a lot of good groups out there who refer quite a bit of business to each other. Again, there's no one method that's perfect. However, when it comes to networking groups, what often happens is that a member will end up spending significant amounts of time and money while seeing little to no results. Most sign-up fees range anywhere from $600 to $1,000 annually. Plus, members pay for lunch each week and end up investing at least an hour and a half of their time to attend the weekly meeting without receiving an ounce of business. This time could be used on other prospecting opportunities.

I've known too many business owners who have been involved in networking groups and haven't gotten a dime out of it. While they have benefitted from the relationships they've built over time, (that you could argue are priceless), it's rare for most business owners to see a significant R.O.I. from attending networking groups. Other challenges with networking groups and specifically anyone offering a high-end product or service are the people you meet at these networking groups and the people they introduce you to who may not exactly be your ideal qualified prospect.

Members of networking groups often grow increasingly frustrated, because they attend weekly meetings, and spend time and money without gaining an ounce of business. I know that as a business owner, marketer or sales professional, your time is perhaps the most valuable asset you have, and so you need to think about how and where you want to apply that asset.

There's one more prospecting method which I haven't personally experienced, but that I do know works for some people: the door knock. Knocking on doors has been around for decades upon decades. Door knocking includes getting in a car, taking the time to show up unannounced, and hoping to get in front of the decision maker for just a sliver of a moment so you can catch their interest. I hear about this all the time. People go to Krispy Kreme, stock up on donuts, and try to get appointments with their ideal prospects.

With the competitors down the street, and all the other companies offering something similar to your product and/or service, as well as all the other XYZs in your industry and your market, when you door knock, you end up doing the exact same thing. As a result, you risk becoming just another commodity and lose any competitive advantage you had. Not to mention the decision maker isn't even in half the time.

You might get a "thank you for the donuts," that the gatekeeper will likely begin enjoying right after you leave. The decision maker might even grab one when he or she gets back from a "meeting." You, on the other hand, end up waiting for that call back which never happens. Before long, you realize you've just wasted your entire afternoon without getting a single appointment and even if you did get an appointment, you might find out the prospect is completely unqualified. So, that appointment turns into a colossal headache, as well as a waste of time and energy. And then there are the prospects who think that just because they have a meeting with you, they owe it to themselves to shop around and commoditize your services.

At the end of the day, if you're doing the same thing that everyone else is doing, you risk commoditizing your business. That's another thing to keep in mind. All these methods we've just covered: the cold calling, cold emailing, networking groups, paying for mailers, in-person visits; they're all things that have become largely commoditized and methods that decision makers have come to expect, and in many cases, resent.

While these methods do work to an extent, if you're looking for a new way to consistently generate appointments with qualified prospects, then there is no better solution, dollar for dollar, than what we're going to talk about inside the pages of this book. I'll now share a little bit of my story and what has qualified me to put together this definitive guide to LinkedIn marketing.

My background with LinkedIn and even my background in the field of marketing started when I was a college student. I had heard that LinkedIn was a place where I needed to be. Even though I was a little reluctant at first, I logged on and built a profile.

My family and I moved to the U.S. when I was 18 months old from a country on the eastern border of Russia called Lithuania. I was fortunate enough to grow up with technology and in the first generation to have social media. Like most kids my age, I started on Myspace. I signed-up for a Facebook account right around the time I started high school.

I quickly became accustomed to social media and was very familiar with various platforms at a young age. LinkedIn however, was a different story. But I started to grasp what it was about through a fortunate experience I had as a college student when I started a new fraternity chapter at my university.

I attended Georgia Southern University in Southern Georgia. I like to refer to it as the Harvard of Southern Georgia. Of course, I say so jokingly, because the other schools, colleges, and universities in Southern Georgia aren't much to write about. Georgia Southern is a school of about 20,000 plus students located in a little town called Statesboro.

When I was in school and first created a LinkedIn profile, I conducted a search on LinkedIn for people across the nation who were in or had been involved with the fraternity I had joined. To my surprise, most of these people I requested a connection with would accept my invite just because we had a shared connection or were both in the same fraternity. These new contacts became a part of my LinkedIn network.

This initially blew my mind, because a lot of them were business owners, high-level executives, and even CEOs, and they were just accepting my connection requests. I was a little guy going to school at the Harvard of Southern Georgia, but I began to realize there could be quite a bit of potential on LinkedIn. One day, I decided to look for new opportunities and I thought that LinkedIn might be a good place to do that. After sending out a few messages to different people, I received a reply from a gentleman who owned a company in Austin, Texas.

He and I had never met, and I didn't think much of the connection to begin with. At first, I only knew that he had the word "CEO" in his title and saw that he had been a member of the same fraternity I was a part of. He and I had a phone call, and I did some work for him and his online company. That was my first experience using LinkedIn to make money.

Just as I was about to finish school, I decided it would be a good idea to travel across the country and move to Vegas.

People often ask me, "Why Vegas?" I just say I had a lot of opportunities. I really had a gut feeling. I still live in Vegas. It's sunny every day, and I like it a lot.

Anyway, I moved out to Vegas and low and behold, I ended up working in sales. At the time, I was working in sales for a software company, and it was my first time selling strictly B2B. I worked for an international software startup, so no one had any idea who we were, what we did, and specifically why they should listen to our pitch. We were going after a couple of different verticals, and it was my job to generate leads, book appointments and turn those appointments into closes.

As a one-man sales team who also did a lot of the marketing, I had to wear many hats. And I know that's part of the reason why my first 30 days on the job were horrendous. I think I booked only one or two appointments in the first month, and the rest of the time was awful because I spent between 6-8 hours a day cold calling.

Since the calling lists were pre-made for me, I did plenty of smiling and dialing. Oftentimes, I wouldn't even get in front of the decision maker, and I was a more than proficient cold caller. I had my script down, sounded smooth, knew what I wanted to say, yet even my preparation and practice didn't matter because I wasn't getting results. After frustration upon frustration, I knew there had to be another way to improve my numbers. That's when I had the big realization.

I started to think about the success I had experienced with LinkedIn. After I had first arrived in Vegas, I connected with several executives and decision makers, some of whom I had an opportunity to sit down and network with for the sole reason that we were connected on LinkedIn. So, it made sense to give LinkedIn marketing a try to generate sales appointments for the software startup.

In the first week of marketing on LinkedIn alone, I started seeing as many and then more results than I had seen from the previous 30 days of cold calling. Not only were potential prospects accepting my requests, but usually, they wanted to engage further in the conversation. LinkedIn also served as a good follow-up to the other cold calling and emailing campaigns we ran. So, I started to develop systems and specific methods as I learned more about marketing on the platform.

Shortly after that, I started going out and networking more in the community. At in-person networking events, I discovered something intriguing. For some reason, I had assumed that everyone knew what I knew about marketing on LinkedIn. To my surprise, I found that the local business owners had almost no idea about the strategies and techniques I was implementing.

One thing led to another, and I took on my first couple of clients who were local business owners and in the B2C industry. Since the strategies I'd implemented in the B2B space appeared to be so underutilized, I remember thinking right before I signed them that in a local market for B2C, it would be much easier and quicker to find success marketing on LinkedIn. It sure was. Within weeks, my clients started seeing results simply by using LinkedIn in a new way and through implementing a few uncomplicated strategies. Back then, I was still very much developing and refining many of the strategies I'll share with you in this book.

Since that time, I've worked with clients in multiple industries across the U.S. I've been fortunate enough to speak and be interviewed on various platforms and publications and have worked with CEOs, multimillionaires, best-selling authors, information marketers, real estate agents, loan officers, financial advisors and in the B2B and B2C sector.

Having worked with all sorts of clients across all sorts of different verticals, what I've realized is that these strategies, the same ones which you'll be reading about in this book, are still very much unknown to most of the business world, and they're still highly effective. What I'm about to share with you is truly a new way of using LinkedIn than most people are accustomed to.

The analogy that I'd like to make for the concepts in this book is blue ocean marketing.

Picture this. The business space is made up of two completely different oceans. The red ocean is filled with bloodthirsty competition. There are sharks everywhere; it's brutal. Every second is a struggle for survival, and everyone is trying to compete for the highly limited resources available. This red ocean is the epitome of a scarce space to play in. What this book talks about, which reflects the truth of LinkedIn marketing and marketing in general, is that most businesses and most sales professionals are still playing in the red ocean. That's why it's become so challenging. That's why there is so much stress, and why there is so much frustration when it comes to solving your biggest challenge of getting in front of qualified prospects. We've talked about the red ocean marketing mentality in the previous pages. It's the one still filled with cold callers, door knockers, people attending networking groups, etc. These are all very much red ocean marketing and prospecting strategies.

Let's talk about the blue ocean for a second. The blue ocean is a completely different place. It's peaceful. The water is clear blue; you can just sit there and gaze through its transparency with no one around you for miles. It's a calm, radiant, blue ocean where you are the only option. Your business is the only business around.

That's the kind of environment you want to play in as a marketer. You want to take advantage of blue ocean marketing. LinkedIn for most industries, especially if you're in the B2C space, and even if you're in B2B it's largely true as well, provides a blue ocean marketing opportunity, because so few people know how to utilize the right way to leverage LinkedIn. This means very few of your competitors have any idea of how to dive in and use those specific strategies to generate appointments with qualified prospects. When working with clients, a lot of what I teach about LinkedIn marketing is finding ways to use blue ocean marketing through marketing on LinkedIn.

Now that we've covered old-school prospecting methods and blue ocean marketing, we can begin to talk some more about LinkedIn itself. LinkedIn is a professional social network, and the company has been around since the mid-2000's. When I first meet potential clients, and when people initially reach out and ask about working with me, I'll often hear something like this.

"It's funny, I've been on LinkedIn for so many years, and I haven't gotten an ounce of business off it. Why is that?"

Since that's a question I'm asked all the time, it's only appropriate that I address it here in this book. After all, that same question may have been going through your mind when you started reading. Maybe that's even why you're reading in the first place.

Let me explain it this way. The old way of using LinkedIn has been all about using it as a resume. Many LinkedIn users only have LinkedIn accounts as a formality. Someone told them it would be a solid idea for them to be on LinkedIn, and so they're on LinkedIn because everyone else appears to be there. What some business owners, marketers, and sales professionals are starting to realize, however, especially those who have just been using LinkedIn as an online resume, is that LinkedIn has so much more potential than they expected.

And if you're reading this, I know you're starting to realize the same thing. You can position yourself as an expert, generate leads, increase your referral networks, build referral streams, and attract more high-end clients through marketing on LinkedIn.

With so many possibilities out there, many of which we will be covering right here in this book, it's time to identify and clarify the outcome you want to reach through your LinkedIn marketing efforts. The big advantage of marketing on LinkedIn that I'd like to help you achieve would be to transform your LinkedIn presence into a lead, referral, and appointment-generating machine.

That's another reason why I wrote this book. In the past, plenty of business owners and sales professionals, even marketers on LinkedIn have had challenges using LinkedIn. Many people grew frustrated with the difficult navigation and user interface. A few even abandoned LinkedIn altogether.

You're probably in the same boat. If you're reading this, then you've probably been a bit frustrated with LinkedIn and your lack of results. If that's you, then you're in the right place. I'll show you a new way to use LinkedIn and help you to uncover pointed strategies to create opportunities. It's time to start playing in the blue ocean and achieve the kind of success you want that is beyond your wildest imagination.

It's time to dive in.

Chapter Two: Impeccable Timing

There has never been a better time than now to start using LinkedIn to grow your business. As you read this book, a variety of factors have been taken into consideration to allow you to take advantage of the information so you can create the perfect combination to use as a business owner, marketer, or sales professional. Here's exactly what I mean.

The first colossal event to take place for the LinkedIn enterprise recently, happened in December 2016. Of course, sooner or later this event will date this book. Microsoft, THE Microsoft, went ahead and purchased LinkedIn for a whopping 26 billion dollars and some change. Ask yourself this question: *Why would Microsoft, a huge company that has been around for a long-time relative to its competitors, have purchased LinkedIn out of all the social media platforms it could have potentially acquired?*

It's time for us to talk about the social media game. While I understand you might not be proficient at social media, you might not be an expert, and you might not even like social media, understanding what I'm about to explain to you will help things make a lot more sense. Here's how social media websites make money. And as I explain this process, think about the social media websites you use most.

We all know about Facebook and Google. But these sites are different. Google operates as a search engine more than a social media website. Then there's YouTube, which mostly functions as Google's social media platform. Don't forget about Google Plus, Instagram, Pinterest, Snapchat, and the many other up-and-coming social media companies.

Here's the question: *How do these websites actually make money?* You know they are free to use for the most part. Even LinkedIn is free unless you have a premium account.

These websites are constantly striving to add active users, because it makes them money. The more active a social media site's user base is, the more time the user base spends engaging on the website. To these social media sites, active users mean more advertisers, which translates into the ability to charge a premium for advertising. The way these social media platforms primarily make money is through selling advertising, and I'm sure you've scrolled through your Facebook feed and even your Instagram or LinkedIn feeds and seen what an ad looks like.

For social media companies to be successful and increase revenue, they need to make money through selling advertising. The better the user experience, the more effective advertisement usually is on a specific platform. That's the real key that permits these companies to thrive and prosper. Microsoft has been falling a little bit behind Facebook and Google since Facebook and Google, at the time of this book, are the predominant social media platforms and predominant Internet companies in the world.

The lagging Microsoft decided it was time to make a big change. They purchased LinkedIn for $26.2 billion with the agreement they would remain fairly hands off the day-to-day operations. Instead, they would provide support, direction, and even help LinkedIn with financial resources.

In short, Microsoft saw an opportunity on LinkedIn, probably like the opportunity you're reading about in this book. Microsoft saw that LinkedIn had over half a billion users across the world in THE professional social network. In LinkedIn, Microsoft saw an opportunity to engage these professionals, attract more advertisers to the site, and make their unique presence felt.

Since that purchase, so many things have already changed. At the start of 2017, LinkedIn implemented the biggest change to its interface and design since its inception in the mid-2000's. If you compare LinkedIn now versus the LinkedIn of 2016, you'll see instantly how the design and user interface look completely different. The new user interface is a lot sleeker and easier to navigate.

That's a frustration so many users used to have with LinkedIn, that the old interface appeared difficult to understand and maneuver. With the new interface, it has never been easier to navigate across LinkedIn and take advantage of some of its features as vehicles for communication and connection.

There were other major changes that came with the new interface. Number one, you'll note the chat box feature. As a LinkedIn user, you now have the power to directly reach a decision maker on their cell phone through chat. Since most people use Internet and social media on their mobile devices these days, LinkedIn has given you the ability to send your message to a decision maker's cell phone. Of course, this isn't a reason to start writing the "perfect pitch" which could be taken as spam that you would send in copious amounts to decision makers. That's not a good idea.

We'll talk in a later chapter about the how-tos of pitching and prospecting on LinkedIn. For now, just be aware that you now have the power to completely get past the gatekeeper and reach that decision maker's cell phone through the chat box feature. The older version of chat used to be a weird mix of email and instant messaging, and now it's a complete chat box. It has also become easier to navigate LinkedIn searches and apply segmentation to targeted audiences. More to come on that later.

While we're on the topic, we might as well talk about the state of the LinkedIn user base. Who spends the most time on LinkedIn? While these stats will date themselves in the future, at the time of the writing of this book about a quarter of LinkedIn's user base is highly active. Everyone else is defined as a more or less casual user, meaning the most active LinkedIn users are often C-level executives, key influencers, and decision makers who use the site to build business connections, learn new information, and engage with relevant and value-filled content.

Business owners, marketers, and sales professionals would be wise to start considering the potential of reaching the exact influencers and key decision makers they're looking for. Not only can this be done on a one-to-one basis, but there are also several strategies you can use to reach audiences at scale and automate parts of these processes. Are you starting to see the potential that LinkedIn could have for you when it comes to turning your LinkedIn presence into a lead-generating and appointment-generating machine? Welcome to the new way of using LinkedIn.

Millennials, believe it or not, are the fastest growing demographic on LinkedIn. Many millennials have gone through a similar experience to the one I shared with you in the first chapter. They have gone to school, wanted to be successful and were told to create a LinkedIn profile. For millennials, there's some bias when it comes to LinkedIn. That bias is this: My generation perceives LinkedIn to be something that's more authoritative when compared to other social media.

When many Millennials come across something on LinkedIn, even a marketing messages, they treat it much more seriously than messages on other social media platforms. That means they give the content or message they see on LinkedIn more time and attention. I'm sure you've seen the flooding of ads on Facebook and other social media platforms. Amidst all the chaos and competition for millennial attention, it's difficult to envision an easier place than LinkedIn to get your message across to this group and ensure they will pay it greater attention than if they saw it elsewhere.

Millennials, the fastest growing demographic on LinkedIn, are beginning to realize that there are tremendous opportunities. You have a chance to reject the old way of using LinkedIn, the glorified resume format, and start distinguishing yourself, your business, and your brand through LinkedIn marketing.

Another reason why your timing is impeccable right now for marketing on LinkedIn is that everybody else is talking about marketing on Facebook. Just as we covered blue ocean marketing in the previous chapter, let's consider marketing on Facebook from that perspective.

I see everyone starting to run ads on Facebook. As a marketer, this is slightly amusing, because when I think of effective marketing, I think of zigging and zagging. When you're marketing, regardless of your industry, it's usually a smart idea to zag when others are zigging and zig when others are zagging. Currently, everyone is zigging in the direction of Facebook as well as Instagram marketing, and very few companies at this point are marketing heavily and marketing effectively on LinkedIn.

If you're a business owner, marketer, or sales professional, it's a golden opportunity to hop on the LinkedIn marketing bandwagon right now. Become an early adopter before LinkedIn gets saturated and flooded with copycat marketing messages. By reading this book and implementing the strategies we talk about, you'll be way ahead of the curve.

People, including your competition, are about to start paying much more attention to marketing on LinkedIn. Now, more than ever, this is your window of opportunity to cash in. There will never be a better time to use marketing on LinkedIn as a new way to generate appointments, find leads and grow your brand and business than right now.

Another thing about marketing on LinkedIn is that most of your competition is completely clueless about the opportunities available let alone how to take advantage of them effectively. This is true whether you're a mom and pop boutique, director of marketing at a large company, or a real estate agent with over 15,000 other licensed agents in your direct market. Most of your competition still thinks of LinkedIn as a place to post a resume instead of as an opportunity-rich place to find fresh business. If you're taking notes, write this down. The time to implement what you learn in this book is now!

If you're someone who's looking to transact business with high-end clients and people who have money, you should be actively marketing on LinkedIn. If you're someone who would like to be perceived as an expert instead of a commodity, then you should be actively marketing on LinkedIn. It's time for me to show you how. If you're ready to take things a step further, I can help you to develop a customized, step-by-step strategy for maximizing ROI from LinkedIn marketing. I highly recommend you visit Linkedleads.Us/Consultation so you can learn more about applying to work with me.

Chapter Three: Systematize or Stagnate

I'm a guy who likes systems. If you're in business and/or in sales, we could probably predict the levels of success you have the potential to reach by the systems that you have or don't have in place. This is especially true when it comes to marketing. Many business owners and sales professionals are still leaving their marketing and lead generation to chance. When you implement a lot of the old-school strategies we talked about early on, you're leaving your results up to chance. Leaving results up to chance is a stressful way of feeding your family.

Leaving things up to chance also appears to be one of the identifying traits of business owners when it comes to LinkedIn. Even people who have received a piece of business or two from LinkedIn are still often left scratching their heads. It doesn't matter that they received those pieces of business from LinkedIn, they usually don't know how to repeat their success.

You need systems in place that can guarantee predictable results. What if you could get predictable appointments on a consistent basis and through a system you installed? This would be a system you and your team could replicate day in and day out. That's really where you want to get to when you use marketing on LinkedIn. This is what I show clients how to accomplish when we work together.

Let me give you my four-step system for LinkedIn marketing. It's a system, which when implemented effectively, can be applied to just about any business. And maybe at this very moment, you think that all of this sounds great but won't quite work for your business, because your business is different. When I hear those words from potential clients, they usually turn out to be the exact clients who start experiencing the quickest and most consistent results.

If you're saying that this won't work for your business, then guess who else is saying that? That's right, your competition. Think of the people who are trying to market to the same or similar audiences. Guess what they're likely not doing? If you do think your business really is different, I encourage you to give this system a try. You'll be surprised at how effectively it works for your business.

W. Clement Stone was a gentleman who lived in the 1900's and was considered by many people to be wildly successful.

He grew his insurance brokerage to seven, eight, maybe even nine figures. W. Clement Stone wrote several books including the one he collaborated on with Napoleon Hill. As you probably know, Napoleon Hill was the author of *Think and Grow Rich*, a classic and still highly popular self-help book. The difference between Hill and Stone was that Stone remained wealthy throughout his life and died without losing his fortune.

Hill, on the other hand, did not. Napoleon Hill was more of an interviewer. In one of Stone's books titled *Success Systems That Never Fail,* he put an emphasis on ensuring success systems were in place for every part of his business. These were successes that didn't fail and produced predictable results. How does the story tie into what we're talking about when it comes to LinkedIn marketing and marketing in general?

The simple answer is what you want to have on LinkedIn are success systems that never fail. Let me give you my success system that never fails for marketing on LinkedIn. It's the same system I cover in-depth in my on-demand training programs and when working with clients. Here it is.

The system starts with optimal profile refinement. In other words, you're working to transform your profile from a resume into a magnet that's attractive to potential clients and referral partners. Let's be clear. We're not talking about turning your profile into the Mona Lisa. You're looking to achieve a profile that will position you as the absolute authority in your field and the premier expert in your space.

Think of the premier expert as the person people feel compelled to go to for questions, the person the media wants to interview, someone you know is a solid business person who more people want to get to know, like and trust. As crazy as it sounds, refining your LinkedIn profile can and will help you move toward achieving all these things, too (when done effectively.)

The second step to the system is content creation and distribution. LinkedIn offers a variety of ways to produce content, many of which we'll be talking about later in this book. For now, take a moment to consider that through content, you can reach hundreds to thousands of people at one time and get these people not only to start seeing you as the expert and premium authority we talked about but also to develop an awareness and interest for the products or services you offer. Oftentimes, you'll be able to touch qualified prospects at scale through content marketing on LinkedIn instead of hounding or bombarding them.

You won't have to be a content wizard to successfully implement content marketing on LinkedIn either. Remember, we're all about strategies which can be simple yet highly effective. In fact, I'll give you some proven strategies and systems later in this book you can leverage to start making content marketing ridiculously easy.

The third step involves using power partners and your current clients. Think about the types of people you'd like to receive referral business from. These are people, especially if you're in real estate, mortgages, or a B2C industry, who are already doing business with and are already known, liked and trusted by your ideal clients.

How powerful would you and your business become if you were able to tap into their networks and have these people send you referrals on a consistent basis while also being willing to expose you to their books of business consistently? LinkedIn marketing offers you that opportunity. You can also start using some of your current clients and tap into the entire Rolodexes of their networks. In case you don't know what a Rolodex is, (and I've personally never used one), they're essentially boxes people used to use to store all the information of the people in their networks. A lot of Rolodexes would store business cards. You now have the ability to tap into entire networks of your current and former clients and to reinforce yourself as the expert who they already know, like and trust.

The fourth step applies more specifically to B2B, but can still apply to B2C. We're talking about strategically prospecting and engaging potential prospects, about discovering potential prospects on LinkedIn who are qualified to do business with you, about systematizing your leads into lists, segmenting your approaches, and engaging prospects in such a way that they'll want to have a deeper conversation, book an appointment, feel comfortable making an offer, and eventually make the decision to invest in your products or services.

Once again, the four-step system I've just introduced you to includes optimal profile refinement, content creation and distribution, using power partners and clients, and strategic prospecting and engagement. When it comes to marketing on LinkedIn, this is a success system that never fails. When you apply the system and effectively implement each of the steps, you will find yourself consistently generating new appointments and growing your business through LinkedIn marketing. Now that I've given you an outline of the system, let's dive into refining your LinkedIn profile. If you'd like to take your marketing on LinkedIn to a new level, I highly recommend that you visit Linkedleads.Us/Consultation and apply to learn more about working with me.

Chapter Four: LinkedIn Profiles: The Billion Dollar Question

When people ask what kind of changes I would recommend they make to their LinkedIn profiles, or how they can make their profiles stand out and look different from the competition, I usually say one thing right off the bat before giving them an answer. I'll warn you, my reply will sound super simple, yet it's something that 99 percent of the profiles I have seen on LinkedIn completely fail to do.

Before we get into what that blind spot is, I also want to point out there are a lot of profiles on LinkedIn that look like what I call "cookie-cutter profiles." An appropriate analogy might be that we could take a LinkedIn profile, and switch it with the name of a competitor; we could switch their photos, and it would look like there wasn't a difference. Let's say you're a loan officer, for example. We could take another loan officer in the same city where you are located, plug their name and photo into your profile, and it will look exactly the same. If what you're reading applies to your current LinkedIn profile, you now have an opportunity to start separating yourself and to do it rather quickly.

Back to the first thing I usually ask people, a billion-dollar question: *What would my audience do?* When it comes to marketing on LinkedIn, and when it comes to marketing in general, *you have to start thinking like your audience.*

Taking that one action will result in the construction of a successful and effective profile. If we were to look at your profile right now, and you were to ask me, "Do you think I'm making the most of this?" the first thing I would have you do is consider the question above. If you visit Linkedleads.Us/Quiz, there's also a free quiz you can take to learn exactly how your profile stacks up against the competition.

Really think about if your profile is the best version it can be for your potential audience, no matter whoever it is you're trying to reach. We're about to cover a few of the most important elements when it comes to distinguishing your profile. When in doubt, go back to the question of what your audience would think and do after visiting your LinkedIn profile.

A good starting point is discussing pictures and photos on LinkedIn. You'll notice on LinkedIn, most people have a headshot, which is acceptable. You want to have a professional looking picture on LinkedIn, even though there are certain elements that apply to a headshot or apply to a photo that either make it effective or make it a questionable photo. The photo of you on LinkedIn needs to be a photo of you. You should not have anyone else in your LinkedIn photo: not your kids, not your dog, not your wife, girlfriend, not your cats, or anyone or anything else.

Your photo should be a picture of you, and it should be bright so people can see your facial features. That's an important factor. You want other people to see your face and your eyes. Lighting is important as well. Make sure you have a well-lit background so people can see your features without having to wonder or squint.

One thing which makes me laugh is seeing a LinkedIn photo, or any social media photo on a personal profile, that's a company logo. A lot of business owners and sales professionals, even marketers, have a seemingly brilliant idea that must sound something like this, "What if I just put my logo as my photo? Won't that get me more exposure?"

When people on LinkedIn are there for business, they want to build a business relationship with a person before building it with a brand. And that's how a lot of social media marketing happens, even on a larger scale. We're in this age where the know, like, and trust factor has never been more critical to understand and embrace. It's imperative to build relationships with people who we do business with.

And so, people who use company logos as their photos are completely negating the fact that people want to build a personal relationship with the person behind the company logo. It pays to be a person and an individual when you connect with others on LinkedIn instead of trying to represent the company. This is how you will get your audience to respond. *What would your audience do?* There's that question again. Your audience would respond to an individual rather than someone who has a company logo as their photo. It's one of those silly mistakes, and if you currently have a company logo as your photo, it's time to take a minute and fix it.

The LinkedIn cover photo is a highly underutilized part of many LinkedIn profiles. It's a unique opportunity for you to brand yourself and even brand your company. Visit

Canva.com, and find the exact layout that will be the right size and will be simple to design even by yourself. Canva is a free website and a snap to use. If you go to my profile, you'll see my cover photo, which I made in Canva. Check it out to get a better idea of what I mean. You can also include a call to action inside the cover photo, and have your visitors click into a specific place where you'd like them to go. For maximum return, make sure that place links to what's called a landing page where you'll be able to collect information from potential leads.

Now, it's time to talk about finally trashing that resume. Our plan is to turn your profile into something tailored for your specific audience. Start by establishing yourself as an expert. Position yourself as the authority in your field through your profile. In the next chapter, we'll talk about some specific tactics to help you do so. For now, think about your profile serving as an advertisement for you and for the value you offer to your audience.

No matter your industry, realize the importance of positioning yourself as the expert. You'd like people finding you on LinkedIn to want to do business with you instead of recruiting you right? Then it's time to start making that apparent in your profile. Headhunting happens to a lot of people, especially in the real estate industry, and if you're in real estate, you can probably relate to this. I bet you get pitched on a regular basis by recruiters who are looking at your profile.

This is annoying and drives many people in the industry crazy. Often, recruiters will merely copy and paste templated messages. Thankfully, there's a way around that, and that is to not accept the request, as you also eliminate any consideration that your profile could be interpreted as a resume. Then again, as we discussed, you don't want to be like everyone else. Work instead toward a profile that compels people to think through your expert positioning: *They're the absolute expert, the absolute authority. That person is the one I want to get to know, like and trust. That's someone I want to do business with* and potentially refer business to. *That's someone I should keep an eye on.* Yes, you can make all those edits to your LinkedIn profile, and it will begin to work for you. In the next chapter, I'll give you even more detail on how to make those changes.

There's an 80/20 rule when it comes to LinkedIn profiles. Now, you could talk about your accolades, your awards, how great you are. You certainly could talk about you. But 80 percent of your profile should be customized completely to appeal to your audience. Even the information you reveal about yourself should be geared toward that audience to help inspire them to eventually do business with you. You can share a little bit of your personality to distinguish yourself. Talk about why it is you do what you do. Tell your story a little bit.

Here's exactly what to do in the summary, and the experience section. Write two or three sentences of your story and why you do what you do. I guarantee you if you're in business or sales, you have a story. You have a reason why you're in your professional field. So, tell people about it. It's going to make you seem a lot more human and make you a lot more relatable to your audience because people relate far better to someone who's not a company, but who's human. A little 2-3 sentence paragraph long enough to give people the information they want to learn about you.

Think of your profile as a tool that will work for you on a consistent basis. You don't have to maintain it regularly. You can update it, and I encourage people to perform periodic updates. A word of caution on periodic updates, I update mine every so often, because it's good to stay fresh in the game. I'll make tweaks here and there.

Clarify your profile positioning, who your audience is and what you want your audience to do (their calls to action.) You want them to decide that you're someone they can know, like, and trust.

As you edit your profile, you can use another little trick to get more engagement on the actions you are taking. Leave the "Notifications" on. When you leave that feature on, every time you edit your profile, your network gets notified in their LinkedIn newsfeeds that you are editing your account.

Initially, as you are making changes and trying to get on the map more on LinkedIn, you can leave that feature on so people can see the changes you've made. But as you're tweaking and going forward, you will want to turn that option off because the last thing you want to do is drive people crazy (who are potentially going to do business with you) every time you change a period, comma, or a question mark on your profile. So, make sure you enable or disable that function as needed.

Building an effective LinkedIn profile comes down to asking yourself, *what would my audience do?*

Here's another story to better illustrate my point. I was speaking once in front of a group of business owners when a woman raised her hand, and said, "I'm a designer. I want to have this type of photo." She then proceeded to describe the type of photo she wanted to use. The response I gave her is your takeaway. When she asked, "Should I do it?" I said, "Well, let me ask you a question. Would your audience be receptive to that picture?" She said, "No." It was as easy as that. The right decision for her and LinkedIn users lies in the answer to that one particular question you will ask yourself. Get to know your audience and before every change or choice you make, don't forget to ask yourself, *what would my audience do? What would my audience think? How would they react? Would this move them closer or further away from taking the exact action that I want them to take— that at some point I know they're going to be ready to take?*

That's it. That's the basis of your entire profile. It's merely thinking like your audience and creating a profile that magnetizes the people you want to work with, as it repels those you don't want to work with.

In the next chapter, we'll get even more granular into the effective recommendations for building your profile, recommendations that will underscore your position as the absolute trusted expert and authority. If you're curious to see how your LinkedIn profile stacks up against the competition, visit Linkedleads.Us/Quiz to take my free assessment.

Chapter Five: Congratulations, You're an Expert

So, what is the importance of expert positioning? Well, expert positioning is one of the most powerful things you can put to work in your favor as a sales professional, marketer, or business owner. Let me explain. As an expert, people seek your opinion. People will come to you to help solve their problems by buying your products or services. My writing this book to teach you a new way of LinkedIn marketing is an action I took to better position myself as an expert. So, one, you see (or read) my efforts to do that, and two, because I am an expert, I would love to invite you to personally work with me or invest in some of my trainings or programs. I'd even love to come speak to your company or clients. That was much more than merely an opportunity for me to tell you more about my business. You see, I just listed out a few of the benefits that you, too, can realize as you reinforce your perception as an expert.

As an expert, your biggest advantage is losing the fear of being a commodity. When you lose the infamous struggle of the business owner you will start to enjoy fewer instances of price shopping and of people overall, giving you a hard time.

When the expert makes a recommendation, when the expert says something, his or her audience listens. You have to be aware of that as you're establishing your expertise as you're building your LinkedIn profile. You want to be the absolute expert and lead trusted authority. Because why would anyone elect to do business with someone who kind of knows the area when they could do business with someone who has absolute expertise—and who is known for that expertise?

One obstacle you might face as you strengthen your expert profile ranking is upper limits. This is what happens when people start to doubt themselves, and they might wonder, *am I really an expert? Do I really know the industry? I've only been in the industry for 20 years, but my competition across the street has been around for 40 years, so do I have the right to call myself an expert?*

One thousand percent yes, you absolutely can refer to yourself this way, and you can even start doing it now. You're a professional; if you've committed yourself to professionally doing something, no matter if you've been in the business for five years or five days, or for 12 days, or 12 years, you can still call yourself an expert because you've made that commitment. And I can guarantee that you are more knowledgeable than 99.99 percent of the potential prospects who you'll come across in those specific areas of expertise. Yes, you have now been given full permission to consider yourself a true expert in your field. And if you're not an expert, then you have no business being in that field, right? If you haven't committed to becoming an expert, if you haven't committed to becoming a true professional, you really have no business being in that field. So, either way, you are an expert. *It's time to accept that you are an expert.* It's time to become the best of the best. It's time for people to start treating you like an expert during business conversations.

You can use your LinkedIn profile to establish your expertise further as well. I'm talking about really doing some powerful things. Let's talk briefly about content marketing—which we'll explore in greater detail in later chapters. There are two types of content marketing on LinkedIn. There's sharing, and there's shaping. Both will allow you to continue to establish affinity so you can build yourself up as that true expert.

What about the permanent stuff on your profiles? Let's discuss the two most important pieces of your LinkedIn profile: your summary and your headline. Your LinkedIn headline is going to be all over LinkedIn. This means whenever you post something, your headline will follow you. Whenever you comment in a group, your headline comes right along with you. This is why it's so important to progress past resume-oriented headlines. I see so many business owners with a headline that says, "Founder and CEO," or my favorite, "Visionary Entrepreneur." Of course, we've also read "CEO," "Sales Professional," or "Salesman." If you have the title of Salesman in your LinkedIn headline, stop what you're doing, stop reading. Put my book down and change that right now. Your headline choice is that critical. Unless you're a VP of Sales at an organization, or you're a sales trainer, you should not have the word "sales" in your LinkedIn headline. It is going to turn off a lot of your potential clients, and it won't help to establish you as an expert. Nope, but it will make people raise the red flag and say, "Oh, wow. It's a salesman." They will run the other way and not even want to connect with you. So, if you have sales in your headline, again, stop what you're doing, and go ahead and change that. I'll give you a second.

Great. Glad we got that out of the way. What should you put in your LinkedIn headline then? You want to enter phrases and keywords that establish you as an expert in your field. These phrases and keywords should also cause people to think "big picture." You want to find out the right keywords for your industry that would cause people to imagine big picture outcomes. You want to show that your product delivers those outcomes through the use of your phrasing, through the wording inside your LinkedIn headline. You also want to have a statement of intent inside that headline when applicable. Also, if you're looking to grow your referral network, mention that in your headline. If you want to show the value proposition you provide, that you help x attain y, for instance, mention that in your LinkedIn headline, too. LinkedIn gives you a limit of characters you can put in your headline, so you want to make it short enough where you don't overload it, and it's not super-saturated, but you want to make it long enough to convey your keywords. This gives you the advantage of showing exactly how you provide value and it gets your potential clients thinking big picture when it comes to doing business with you.

Make your headline visually appealing. You can do this by using the vertical brackets on your keyboard to separate the key phrases. You don't want to use commas, because it is less appealing. If you're using a PC, hold down Shift and hit the key just above enter, the one with the straight line and the diagonal bracket. Again, you want to really stand out and think authority, think expertise, think about what your audience would be compelled to do. Think about who your audience would want to do business with and get to know, who would fascinate them.

Now, let's talk about your LinkedIn summary. This is the premier place to establish yourself as an expert. I'll give you two techniques right now that will change the game for you in your LinkedIn summary.

Number one, social proof. It's huge on LinkedIn. Social proof is a concept that Robert Cialdini, defines in his book *Influence*. It happens when a third party validates us for whatever it is we're saying or doing. It's not the same to hear how amazing we are from us; it's never as powerful as hearing how wonderful we are from a third party. Show social proof early on in your LinkedIn summary. You can lead with either a testimonial or a quote from a magazine, for example. It's vital that it is something that will automatically capture their attention and cause them to think: *Wow, that's a third party, not just Joe Schmo saying he's great, but people are saying awesome things about that person.* Or, *that caught my attention.* You want to grab their attention with social proof. And there's no better way to do that than in the LinkedIn summary.

Also, to establish yourself as an expert, you want to take people through this process, that is subconscious. We all go through this process when we are about to make the decision of whether or not we want to purchase a product or service. You know the old acronym that stands for Awareness, Interest, Decision, Action. It's a similar path that a LinkedIn user goes on when they read your profile. You want to lead them through this discovery, and one way to do that while you're establishing expertise is by asking questions. It's like conducting a discovery call without making the call. You can start by thinking about the three questions, or the three biggest pain points you know are problematic for your ideal clients. You want to have in your summary, as a leading expert or from whatever your position is, questions chosen to give you the answers you need. Imagine some of the questions your clients might ask you, so when your potential client reads those questions, they'll say, "That person understands me." Or, "That person must know the industry really well." Then they'll figure out it's someone they know, and if they're in the market, then they will want to get to know you.

So, the importance of finding what those three questions will be and listing them out on your summary cannot be overstated. But before we go any further, let me just pause to give you a word of caution about your LinkedIn summary. I teach my clients using my mock profile and perfect profile formulas as well as instruct in programs that complement my consulting. I use symbols to teach people how to make it all make sense. You want to make it aesthetically pleasing. The last thing that you want to do is to make it a big run-on sentence with a flurry of information. This is why you want to use symbols. Symbols are more than emojis or icons. You can use various shapes like stars and diamonds as long as those shapes resonate with your audience. Go ahead and Google some symbols, then copy-paste them in your summary to make it stand out and give it a unique feel. As you are working away in your summary, keep in mind that the goal is to break your summary down into chunks, meaning no more than two or three sentences at one time. That's the rule for chunking your profile.

Everything that I have shared with you so far helps lay the foundation for building your profile. There are also other elements. Keywords start your profile off, and, recommendations are a big asset, too. But the key is to build your expertise.

I worked with a loan officer who's now receiving so many compliments on her profile just because, a) it doesn't look like a cookie cutter profile, and, b) it portrays her as the absolute expert. Her improvements came because she just started applying some of the techniques I taught her.

Before you go all crazy and start making changes everywhere, make sure you go to Linkedleads.Us/Quiz and take my free quiz. You can see where your profile stacks up against the competition. The quiz will give you insight into what you can start changing and implementing right away.

Chapter Six: New-School Networking

Warning, this chapter may be controversial. In fact, a lot of people reading it will disagree with me. If you're someone who does, that's a personal choice, but know that what I'm about to describe has been highly effective for numerous clients across the nation, across the world, and it has changed the game for people in my LinkedIn network as well. It continues to be effective for me to this very day. What I am about to share with you is something I personally utilize and that I've experimented with a lot. I've seen and read up on multiple approaches, and this is by far the most effective approach to networking on LinkedIn. I classify it as a new-school way of networking in general.

I recently read an article about how people are using LinkedIn the wrong way. Now, the founder of LinkedIn, a gentleman by the name of Reid Hoffman, was quoted in the article saying he originally intended LinkedIn to be a place where people could connect with people they already knew. His aim was for LinkedIn to be a tight-knit professional network. Of course, that's not the way 99 percent of LinkedIn users are using the site today. In fact, let's do a test. Stop for a second and think, do you know or do you have a relationship with every single connection in your LinkedIn network? I can almost guarantee that you don't...my prediction is that most people reading this book aren't using LinkedIn like that. I also predict that they haven't been using LinkedIn like that for a while, if at all. You see, part of the draw to marketing on LinkedIn is your ability to go wide. I enjoy scrolling through my LinkedIn feed and seeing content from people I'm not directly connected to. The content sharing algorithm is part of what makes LinkedIn so unique.

What I mean is, if you scroll through your LinkedIn feed, a large percentage of the posts and content you see is because someone in your network engaged with that piece of content. For example, if you and I are connected, and I like an article then you might see that article I liked that was shared by someone who's not even in your immediate network. In this way, you'll be able to start engaging with a person you don't even know. The algorithm on LinkedIn is amazing when it comes to interaction like that.

This means that if you're only accepting connection requests from people you already know, you're doing yourself a disservice and missing opportunities to form new business relationships on LinkedIn. This brings to mind a question I get asked a lot: *Should you accept every connection?* Absolutely not. Every person has the option to add a personal note with their LinkedIn request by clicking a little button that allows you to add a note. If the person sending the request hasn't taken the time to customize a message that shows a legitimate reason for wanting to connect, sometimes it's best not to accept the request at all. Because let's face it, they might be a spammer. But before we jump to any decision, let's at least look at their profile. If, after looking at their profile, you see any reason why connecting could be beneficial (unless they're a spammer), accept their request. Even if they do turn out to be a spammer, you can always remove them from your connections. Disconnection is a click of a button away. Because you see, on LinkedIn sometimes you don't know. It's hard to get it right 100 percent of the time. The person who you initially thought might be a spammer could message you saying they want to become a client or a potential referral partner and of course, vice versa.

Here's how I screen my inbound connections. Number one, I visit their profile, and I scroll through their headline; I read their summary, see how many connections they have, and then I make a judgment call. Ask yourself these questions.

Do we have mutual connections? Do they know me? Could they potentially know me? Or, *do they look like a spammer?* If there's not anything fishy, I'll go ahead, and I'll accept their request. That's step two. Number three, I'm going to send a message, and you can swipe this one or write something similar, to the one I use (below.) Remember, I send this message right after I accept their connection request, because we get so busy in the day sometimes we forget the people we have communicated with, so, I make sure I always remember to do this.

I say, "Hi (first name). Thanks for inviting me to join your network. What made you want to connect?"

You can also say it's nice to meet them and thank them for inviting you to join their network if you would like to use a more formal tone.

Do you know why I use this wording?

I'm using a word track that asks them what made them want to connect. If they message me back, they're committing to a reason to want to connect, which means I get to find out exactly what their intention is and I can carry on that conversation further no matter what it is they want. You never know what kind of opportunity it might lead to.

I might also ask, "How'd you hear about me?" because I've gotten some decent publicity across the nation; I've been interviewed in numerous publications. Since I am getting recognition, I've also been able to tap into multiple industries. So, I like to ask, "How'd you hear about me?" Either way, you can ask them what made them want to connect or ask how they heard about you. If they don't respond to your initial attempt at conversation, go ahead and remove them from your connections. It takes no time to break the connection, and if they don't want to engage, you might not want to have them in your network. However, leaving them in your network also won't hurt because if they choose to engage with your content at some point, using their first degree connections (the connections who said yes to either your connection request or who've sent you a connection request that you've accepted) then your first degree connections would be exposed to your content as well. In case you were wondering, second-degree connections are defined as people with whom you have at least one mutual connection. Third-degree connection means you interact with someone with whom you have zero mutual connections.

Going wide on LinkedIn doesn't hurt, especially if you're a business owner or a sales professional. In fact, I encourage you to go wide. You'll even notice that some people refer to themselves as L-I-O-N-S or lions on LinkedIn, which stands for LinkedIn open networkers. These are often the best people to connect with. Especially if they fit the vertical where you'd like to market. Because they're open to new relationships. They're open to connecting. They're open to engagement. Do you have to identify yourself as a lion if you are going wide? That's entirely up to you. I don't do it. To me, it seems a little bit corny, but to each his own. If you want to include the title of lion in your profile, by all means, go crazy. I'm open to networking and will accept no spammers.

Some people, who are still wrapped up in the old-school LinkedIn perception, might think open networkers on LinkedIn are not operating with integrity. What these people are failing to realize is the value LinkedIn has to offer. Think about it like this: When it comes to networking, when it comes to marketing, even when it comes to building relationships, we were all strangers at some point. And networking, online and offline, is all about forming new relationships as well as preserving old ones. If you haven't been expanding your LinkedIn network, you've been missing a tremendous opportunity, and it's time to change that right here, right now.

It's time to go wide.

Let me offer you a side note on competition, because this will address another question people ask me. "Is it smart for me to connect with direct competitors on LinkedIn?" The answer depends on the specific industry. Sometimes, your perceived competition can turn into a referral source. Maybe they specialize in a couple of things that you don't or vice versa. Instead of them losing the business, they can get a perk from referring business to you, and you can return the favor. Another benefit of linking to competitors is that if you're someone who follows the strategies I teach and the conversations in my private Disrupting LinkedIn Facebook group...which you can join completely free...you'll quickly realize how clueless most of your competition truly are when it comes to LinkedIn marketing. When you connect with them, you can get a feel for what your competition are doing and what they aren't doing.

I was asked this question by a client who only wanted to be connected to potential referral partners who would help him work toward meeting his end potential prospects. I told him it was a good approach. And I would still want to go wide to make sure he could tap into other people's networks. If you know someone who's not a potential referral partner or not a potential client, they may still have people within their network, a network you can review on LinkedIn, who you might want to meet. You might be missing out on an opportunity if you don't go wide. So, you really have nothing to lose.

Here's the rule of thumb. If you don't see any benefit at all in connecting with your perceived competitor, simply don't accept their request. Also realize that the LinkedIn groups you want to be a part of should be groups full of potential prospects and referral partners, instead of individuals who do exactly what you do. I see so many real estate agents, so many loan officers, who join groups for real estate agents and loan officers. While that's a good plan because you should utilize industry knowledge to learn best practices, chances are those people and businesses aren't going to be your ideal clients and prospects. You want to spend time with people who might go on to do business with you. Join groups full of your potential prospects and referral partners. Not your competitors, not your colleagues in your industry.

The new way of networking on LinkedIn, of going wide, and this new-school networking approach, is the future of networking on LinkedIn. There's a lot of potential, and you never know who you're going to meet. You never know who other people know as well. The six degrees of separation that we talk about, how everyone kind of knows everybody, it's true, and it's never been easier to penetrate into that circle and use that to your advantage on LinkedIn.

The last thing I want to touch on as we wrap this chapter is the story of 150. Once there was an economist whose last name was Dunbar. He had this theory of 150 that thousands of years ago when people lived in tribes and villages, we didn't have an awareness of more than 150 people. So, we attributed our core of 150 as this tribe of people who we knew, liked, and trusted, and everyone was assigned certain roles. As it relates to networking on LinkedIn, you want to go wide and what will happen is that you'll have quality within your contacts. Yes, you'll have the 150 who see most of your stuff, and who engage with you the most, and who you'll end up doing the most business with, but you will also have a chance to think about the relationships you want to build, to work toward having quality as well as quantity. When you use the systems I teach, you will be able to truly realize having both things. In closing, never sacrifice quantity for quality, and never sacrifice quality for quantity. You can have the best of both worlds when connecting with people on LinkedIn when you take this new approach and run with it.

Chapter Seven: How to Never Run Out of Content to Publish on LinkedIn Again

Sitting beside a client one day, we were scrolling through his newsfeed, and I came to an ugly realization about LinkedIn and content marketing on LinkedIn. We were studying how active one of his potential new referral partners was, and we noticed that the person's most recent post had received zero engagements so far. It looked 100 percent inauthentic.

On the surface, this post had looked promising, and the person we were talking about was in the real estate industry, so the post seemed relevant to his target audience. It did link to a blog on another site, and it did have a "catchy enough headline." But as soon as my client saw the post, he immediately chuckled and pointed out just how blatantly obvious it was that this person was paying a third party to post on his behalf.

It was at this point that I realized how obvious those kinds of posts are, especially in a place like the LinkedIn newsfeed. So, not only was this person paying to have a third party write garbage content for them, they were probably paying on a month-to-month basis to generate the exact opposite effect of what the person under contract intended. As a matter of fact, these posts were damaging their credibility and alienating them from their target audience.

I see a lot of people doing this on LinkedIn, especially in the real estate industry or in industries where people are afraid of content marketing, so they spend an exorbitant amount of money paying a third party to post for them. Let me let you in on a little secret. People can tell when it's not you posting. There is a way around it, because you don't necessarily have to be the one posting everything. If you want to outsource that task, you can still do it using the tools I'll identify, and you will be just that much more effective.

A lot of people are afraid of content marketing, (and you may be one of them.) Yet there are some facts you don't know that when you find out, may help you feel more confident. First, there are two types of content marketing. There's sharing, and there's shaping as I've mentioned and which I'll talk about in the next chapter. But for now, let's talk about a very specific way to market content on LinkedIn. By the way, when I say content marketing, all I mean is literally posting content to LinkedIn. You will find there are a lot of ports of content that you can use to post on LinkedIn, and these resources are only getting better over time.

Many people are afraid to use LinkedIn, because they just don't know what to post; they're out of ideas, and it's a headache. You're a business owner, marketer, or sales professional. You've got a million and one things you're juggling already, so the last thing you want to think about is what in the world to post on LinkedIn and how to post it.

My system will give you a shortcut for this problem. I want you to specifically rethink how you think about LinkedIn Publisher, which is the portal blogging platform inside LinkedIn. What you're able to do with LinkedIn Publisher is publish blog-type articles right inside LinkedIn that end up having a super clean and pristine look. Despite being a tool that's available to all LinkedIn users, a very small percentage of LinkedIn users are utilizing LinkedIn Publisher and getting the types of results that we're going to be talking about on a consistent basis.

It's another example of blue ocean marketing, because when you publish on LinkedIn Publisher and when you use the right approach, it boosts your SEO, (your search engine optimization) that comes from having a blog posted within one of the most SEO friendly websites on the planet. LinkedIn and Google get along very, very well. You're also going to allow more prospects to discover you and your company, and right away you're going to distinguish yourself as a highly credible authority in whichever area you'd like to establish expertise. It's just another side benefit, because most of your competitors if they are writing a blog, are posting it on their website and they're struggling to get traffic. LinkedIn will generate traffic for you when you use these strategies that we talk about. I like to think about it as a great way to hack the system and get in front of potential prospects for free.

Since you're going to start publishing now using LinkedIn Publisher, you will also at the same time commit to content marketing. If you've read this far, I think I've persuaded you to at least give it a try. I want to give you my method, my proven system to make sure you won't ever have another moment where you will be without content to post or publish. In the next chapter, we'll talk about different types of content, which content you should be posting and the difference between sharing and shaping content.

Before we get into that system, you need to know about my proven hack that I call the FROGS method. It's my acronym describing my system for posting content, especially when I publish articles on LinkedIn Publisher. I'll usually publish about two articles a week, (some weeks it varies, some I'll do more, some I'll just do one.) It really depends on how I want to align my goals, objectives, and intent for that week. On average, I usually hit two on a regular week, using this method. It's quite simple to do.

The "F" in the FROGS method stands for frequently asked questions, so if you haven't done so already, I recommend you make a list of about 10 to 15 questions that concern the product or service you're offering. These are the questions that are, or could be on the minds of your ideal clients. Again, we're not just thinking about anybody, you're thinking about your ideal clients, the high-end clients, your dream clients who you want to do business with. What are the questions that they most often ask you, or that you know they most often ask businesses such as yours? What will they be likely to ask due to any recent change you, or they, might have undergone? I'm sure there are least a handful of questions that come to the top of your mind right away. So, go ahead, make that list of frequently asked questions. It's going to help you not only on LinkedIn but in your marketing and sales across the board.

Now that you've listed your frequently asked questions, each of them can be used at a minimum to create a separate piece of content. Furthermore, they can become an article on LinkedIn. If you've listed 10 to 15 frequently asked questions, guess what, you now have 10 to 15 new topics for content marketing. You're going to repurpose all these into content on LinkedIn. All you have to do is address each question in an article on Publisher, and guess what(?) you have a new post.

When you use this technique, you'll build and increase your level of trust with your intended audience as you ensure a more efficient and enjoyable sales process. If it's a frequently asked question that happens to be long winded or has multiple parts, that's even better, because now you can break that up into a series of multiple posts or multiple articles which can all be used for content marketing to deliver a ton of value for that intended audience.

The "R" in the FROGS method stands for relevant updates. Regardless of the product or service you offer, I'm sure you make an effort to stay current on the latest trends and news in your industry. Especially the ones that directly affect or can directly affect your clients. Remember we talked about being an expert? That's what experts do; they stay relevant. Chances are your ideal clients don't take nearly as much time as you do to stay up to date with your industry, because they are not experts. You're the expert. Take advantage of this. LinkedIn Publisher is one of the best places to provide expert insights and turn those into relevant updates. Let your ideal clients know about changes taking place either in your industry or within your company. Ideal clients exist inside your specific audience segments, communities or demographics that you may be targeting through LinkedIn marketing when you put content on LinkedIn.

I also encourage you to take your articles a step further, so they contain relevant updates, happening in real time throughout your industry. Then make sure to add in-depth analysis and recommendations.

Let's say you're in the mortgage industry, and rates have gone up by 75 points. Instead of just announcing in your article "rates have gone up," I want you to add some deeper analysis. Talk about how the rates going up have affected your clients and make a recommendation. You can say, "Based on these new rates, here's what I recommend." So, first state the update; second, give your in-depth analysis. That's going to set you up for more success than merely being a news bearer; it's going to help transform you into the expert you know you're already becoming.

If you are in a high-compliance industry, a financial planner, for instance, and I have several clients in this field, then you can make up for any limited analysis by making strong recommendations to your audience to further connect with you. This is the time to use a call to action. When you post the relevant update, extend to your audience that a great thing to do would be to sit down and talk for 20 minutes, or they might like to go to your free workshop.

You want to make a correlation between giving the update and then including the call to action. The next step is either to gather more information or to sit down with you and schedule an appointment. Making an offer when you post an update is a good way to justify the call to action. Of course, you want to stay within compliance, but you're more than capable of doing that in most industries. I am confident you'll be able to spin it and frame it the right way.

Onto the "O" in the FROGS method, which stands for objections. This is one of my favorite ones. Objections often take the form of resistance. These are the obstacles that get in the way of your ideal process and your ideal buying decision. They block people from doing business with you. No matter if you provide the top product or service with features and benefits that blow away the competition, you're still going to encounter specific objections before your prospects make a buying decision.

Why not use these specific objections and pieces of resistance as enriching content? We absolutely will do that. Here's your first step: Let's come up with a list of common objections that you hear on a regular basis about your products or service. Again, if you don't have that list already, it's a great exercise to complete. The goal is to come up with elaborate yet concise explanations that completely discredit and overcome the resistance and objections. You're going to do that for each objection, and each objection can then become its own piece of standalone content, whether it lands on LinkedIn Publisher or is just a piece of content you post in your newsfeed.

Not only will you be able to put out refreshing and useful content that will give value to your audience, but you'll also strengthen your sales process and become even better at handling main objections—because now you can handle them in real time. The other benefit is that you can also refer your prospects to a resource, (which by the way, you've already created because you're the expert) who's going to handle their objections for them and ease that resistance.

The "G" in the FROGS method stands for gold. I love this part of the process. In using this analogy, we talk about practical tidbits, pieces of gold, pieces of value that provide a benefit to your audience. These are often things that your audience can apply almost right away. If you're in a consulting space, your tidbits of practical value are often strategies your audience will find useful. If you're in mortgages, these are insights you're aware of that your audience should be aware of, too. Depending on your industry, these are immediate-acting pieces of gold. You want to make sure these tidbits are actionable, and you want to avoid falling into the trap of using industry lingo.

You should be familiar with industry lingo, because again, you are an expert. You're well-versed with almost anybody you'll meet regarding your industry. I tend to do this as well, devolve into using the jargon, but I've started to double up my efforts not to, because my credibility can take a hit. Avoid those specific terms only industry insiders understand. For example, if I am in the mortgage industry, there are different types of loans. We can get into rates and details, all the technical stuff that's not going to help your audience move forward in the buying process. And this approach will not help you reach your content goals. What you want to do instead is apply analogies and metaphors; these can go a long way. Like what I'm doing here with the FROGS method, I've given you an acronym and a bit of a metaphor, so you can relate as you're reading this and appreciate what I'm sharing. Then you will come back for more, right?

This point is HUGE. Had I gone technical on you and talked about top funnel marketing, bottom funnel marketing, and content marketing along with inbound marketing and segmentation, I would have lost you by now, and you probably wouldn't be reading any more. So, I demonstrated instead what you need to do, which is take technical information and break it down in a way where you can tell a story your audience will understand. You're going to use analogies and metaphors to help you along the way, and you will find your audience will further appreciate the tidbits you share, because all your competition is still using industry lingo. It's confusing to your audience, and it doesn't resonate with them the way your metaphors will.

The last letter of the FROGS method is "S," and it represents the word "series." Think about your favorite TV shows, mini-series or soap operas, if you're into that sort of thing. The best ones keep you coming back for more, don't they? You could do the same with articles on a given topic, or even content that you post on LinkedIn. You could keep your audience coming back for more, too...which would be amazing and fulfill a goal.

If for example, you put out an article that's part of a three-part series on content marketing on LinkedIn, and the next article in the series is scheduled to be released a week from now, you would want to make sure you have a hook at the end. This will ensure your audience returns to read more information from you. To do this, at the end of these articles, you want to give them a little snippet, a sneak preview of what they can expect from the next article. Give your readers a clear day and time for the next publication in the series.

Series work particularly well with long-form types of content. Regular posts that are far shorter don't perform as well, and so you probably won't want to apply this recommendation to those types of content. But certainly, feel free to play around, because different structures will be effective depending on your industry.

In the next chapter, we'll go over the difference between sharing and shaping content, and I'll give you additional resources you can use to find things to post on LinkedIn. I'll also break down some of the content algorithm for you as well. I ask you to remember as you learn about the algorithm that the formula that powers it is ever-changing, just like every other element in digital marketing. If you'd like to learn more about using content marketing to develop marketing assets which will constantly work for your business, go to Linkedleads.Us/Consultation to learn more about applying to work with me.

Chapter Eight: Sharing and Shaping

As you've already read, there are two different types of content on LinkedIn that are presently being used, but really, there are two types of content that are used that apply to all content marketing. I'll break it down for you inside this chapter and show you exactly how to use these components to your advantage.

Sharing content is anything that was not produced by you directly. Sometimes if a company produced it, you could still share it. You will see a lot of this kind of goings on in the LinkedIn feed and on other blogs as well. People share articles, videos, all sort of different things. When it comes to sharing videos on LinkedIn, at the time of this writing, you can only share videos from YouTube. However, live uploads are coming to LinkedIn, and they will be the thing of the future which I'll talk about a little later. I can say this is the direction we are headed with almost 100 percent certainty.

When you are putting stuff out there and sharing, you want to make sure you're posting on a consistent basis. Doing this will give you the most oomph in the LinkedIn newsfeed as of now. What's neat about LinkedIn is that they provide analytics for you. You can see exactly how a post from your profile did, how many views it received, and obviously how many likes and comments it received as well. When you share content, what gets the most views can all be traced back to quality and quantity. Make sure to stay consistent in sharing quality content, and the payoff will be there.

I was working with a client; he put out an article, and it received over 1,000 views. His article did well. LinkedIn even published it across their syndicated platform. I asked him, "Since your article did so well, how many leads did you get out of it?" He paused for a second and then said, "None."

This story drives home the point that you want quality views over quantity views. Just because something goes viral, it doesn't necessarily mean you'll get any business out of it. But if you have views from a targeted audience, that type of engagement will go a long way. You'll be able to use your readers' actions and turn them directly into leads.

The LinkedIn algorithm is a cool thing because, at the moment, people on LinkedIn who aren't in your immediate networks can see your content. If you look at my content on LinkedIn, as an example, and you give my article a like, the people in your LinkedIn network—your first-degree connections—will see some of my content. They'll be able to engage with it, connect with me, enter my marketing funnel, or execute whatever other call to action I'd like them to take. My odds absolutely increase that these events will happen. This is such a powerful thing about LinkedIn and the LinkedIn content algorithm.

The content that works best for me is a simple quote, so I'll find a quote and just post it. I won't even post the image. I'll post a simple quote onto LinkedIn. That's it. I'll attribute it, use one or two lines and I'll share it. Every time I do that, the quote gets anywhere from 10 to 15 actions of engagement and a few hundred views. So, I'm telling you, it might be surprising to post a quote this way, yet it works really well.

What works even better is using human interest, I want to hit home on this point. So, bear with me. LinkedIn content and any social media content, really, thrives on the human-interest element. You can post a photo, which will do well on LinkedIn, but make sure the photo you post is large. It needs to be at least 900 by 900 PX. Make sure the photo is large enough so people can see it, and it will grab their attention as they're scrolling through their LinkedIn newsfeed. You must keep in mind that most LinkedIn users are going to be scrolling on mobile, so it's imperative that you make your photo large.

When we talk about a human-interest post, I mean that you tag someone in a photo and then write a little blurb about it and them. Whether you've accomplished something or just helped a client, in sharing that post, you can even tag the client as well. We'll talk about some ways to get in front of your clients' networks in the next chapter, so stayed tuned, because this is an insider secret I can't wait to reveal to you.

Human interest posts are proven to reach greater virality than other kinds of posts on LinkedIn. I've seen some of the most ridiculous posts receive plenty of engagement. They were simply comprised of a picture of a female or a male, and a short paragraph about them. Again, the picture had good lighting and was large. The paragraph was intriguing. The posts started to catch like wildfires using a combination of these factors. As I said, it's so uncomplicated, but human-interest content performs in the highest percentages on LinkedIn.

You can redistribute content from other places to LinkedIn, too, meaning you can share content to the newsfeed from other places. Now LinkedIn, again, wants users to spend time on the newsfeed, so you'll get the most engagement from content that doesn't drive traffic off LinkedIn. Posts housed in LinkedIn Publisher will give you the returns you want. LinkedIn Publisher is such a useful tool. We'll spend some time talking about that shortly.

The newsfeed on LinkedIn is an interesting place. If you haven't looked at it intensely, take a second. You'll scroll through, see sponsored posts, sure, but you'll also see posts, making up a percentage of posts from people who aren't in your immediate network. As I've explained, you see those posts, because someone in your network has engaged with them. The newsfeed is an impressive force, and quite different from any other social media website.

Now that you know you can share content, it's important to post successfully. I like to build a road map at the beginning of the week and schedule out exactly what will be posted on my personal page and more recently, on my company page. I schedule it out, so I don't have to worry about it every day. Using the FROGS method, I know exactly what will be posted, and this gives me further insight into the kind of things that I'd like to share and should share, that my audience will eat up. Because, again, it all comes back to what your audience would think and making sure you craft content around their needs.

If you want current updates or to know what current event posts have done well, go to Google news and check out some current events that you could share in an article. The keys are to give some of your insights, write a paragraph or two, or a sentence or two for that matter, and then share it. You'll notice trending stories, and articles get the most engagement.

One recent update LinkedIn just made works perfectly when you are writing to capitalize on a trend. On the right-side bar of LinkedIn, you will see business-related articles that are the hot topics. So, if you ever run out of things to post about, or if you want a really, really fresh subject, you can click on those articles, then share some of your insights and don't forget to use the hashtags as well so you will show up in searches.

Hashtags on LinkedIn are a weird thing, because they've come and gone, but then when you look again they're back.

Yes, they are relevant to your traffic. You want to use at least three hashtags when you post so that people can find you, and you'll increase your virality consequently. No matter what LinkedIn decides to do about hashtags going forward, it will never hurt you, so it makes sense to include this to-do in your content marketing. I will say, when you are using writing shaping content for LinkedIn Publisher, (which we'll get into next,) then it's more important to use those hashtags, but for regular post sharing, what you'll want to do is limit your number of hashtags (three is the current best practice) and use them in conjunction with short posts. When you do this, it's a very effective marketing effort.

When it comes to motivational memes and similar content, they have become so over-used and so over-saturated, they don't necessarily have the bandwidth they used to. But you can put a spin on this old practice by framing quotes of yours or quotes from anyone in a meme and then branding it. You especially want to do this if you're in the consulting or marketing space. Share those custom memes on LinkedIn; write little paragraphs when you post each one, and remember to include a nice call to action.

Those are the nuts and bolts of sharing content. The key takeaway for you here is consistency. Consistency leads to quality views. Try to make sure you're posting once a day. And did you know the algorithm is a compounding model, meaning when someone engages with a post the increased visibility takes effect all over again? If I like a post from a year ago, people are going to start seeing that post again. It resets the clock, and it helped me to discover a sneaky little thing to give old posts new life. Let's say you have a post that has three comments on it, and it hasn't gotten any engagement in three months. Go on it and comment; like and reply to one comment, and then do it again in a couple of days. When you do this, you'll put that post back into circulation. It's a neat trick to try with the LinkedIn algorithm.

When you share articles from other websites, LinkedIn won't help you as much in the algorithm. Long form copy works well also, so you can use a lot of words, but you have to space it out, and make it visually appealing.

This brings us to shaping content, and this is really what's going to separate you as well as position you to be the influencer that you know you are. There are two types of shaping content that you can apply to LinkedIn. Number one is LinkedIn Publisher; number two is SlideShare.

LinkedIn Publisher is the blog platform that I mentioned in the last chapter. It's part of LinkedIn, and when you publish something on LinkedIn, it will stay on your profile forever. If you go to my profile, you can see every article that I've published on LinkedIn Publisher right under my summaries. In essence, it becomes a library and a smart place to house your blog. Instead of having a blog on a website and worrying about how to drive traffic to it, I highly encourage you to house your main blog, and your main content marketing through LinkedIn. LinkedIn will put it into circulation, so you'll get eyeballs on it that you wouldn't otherwise receive. And you will get those views for free.

Right now, you can only post on LinkedIn Publisher using a desktop, and it's a sleek platform if you haven't played with it. Look at some of my articles if you'd like a few examples. When you use LinkedIn Publisher, it will help you to really position yourself as the expert.

I've given you loads and loads of topics, I've given you systems for producing content. So, let me give you a few best practices for publishing on LinkedIn as well. Make sure you don't have clumpy paragraphs. No paragraph should be more than three or four sentences. Make sure you bold key points to make it easy on the eyes. These tips are pretty easy to miss, and we're all over the place with our attention spans these days as it is. Make sure your post isn't too long; 1,000 words is a good benchmark, and 2,000 is a solid maximum. Ideally, 200-300 words could be long enough to build a potential article.

Another key to keep at the forefront is your image. I like to use images that are well known and which people can relate to. Make sure to give due credit to the photos you use. When your image is something people experience emotion over, it'll get more people to your article. You want to get them to actually click into and view the article, that's the first component of success on LinkedIn Publisher.

What is even more impactful than the image you use is your headline. There's a great tool out there for headline writing that will help you to better optimize your headlines, and that measures how effective your headline will be using a set of criteria. CoSchedule.com has a free headline analyzer, so you can see how your headlines stack up. I also have an article about it on my LinkedIn profile, so if you are not connected to me on LinkedIn, send me a connection request and check out my post on crafting compelling headlines. There are 12 different templates for writing effective headlines. There's an art to it, and you want to make sure you're doing it as well as you can, because this will influence the number of people who will click on your article.

And here's yet another way to establish expertise. At the end of your LinkedIn Publisher articles, insert a blurb that you can copy and paste in italics. This insertion should be written in the third person about you. Again, if you read my articles you'll see that at the end of each article there is a 2-3 sentence blurb, that's written about me, in the third person, and that further helps establish the expert positioning. This brief little blurb adds legitimacy to your post on LinkedIn Publisher.

Those are some of the best practices I have found through personally using LinkedIn Publisher, but you want to go in there and play around with it yourself. If you'd like some help with LinkedIn Publisher, come take a look at some of my programs, where I will go into much more depth with you. I can help you get exactly the results you're looking for on LinkedIn Publisher, as well as set it up specifically and customize a system for generating leads from Publisher. When we do this, we will put those leads inside your marketing funnel. That's where I get a lot of the leads I receive on LinkedIn, right through content marketing on LinkedIn Publisher.

Now, let's get into SlideShare. SlideShare is a fairly new tool LinkedIn recently incorporated. It's a platform where you can upload presentations directly. This also lends credibility to your positioning as an expert. If you have slides or presentations you've already completed for your business that are educationally based, you can upload them. When you do, use a lot of hashtags. Follow these steps, and you can categorize these presentations to reach the top of the category easily.

If you're in the real estate industry, you would use the tags for your area as you upload the SlideShare. That way when people search for those keywords on LinkedIn, looking for real estate in Tampa, Florida, for example, your SlideShare's likely going to be one of the first pieces of content that come up if you've done it the right way.

If you have calls to action embedded inside that SlideShare, then you'll be able to generate leads, which will cause your audience to act. SlideShare's pretty straightforward. It's a part of LinkedIn. You can upload presentations directly. Your biggest takeaways for SlideShare content are to include a call to action and your keywords, which will improve your ranking.

In the next chapter, we'll talk about opinions and eyeballs as well as endorsements and a lot of other great stuff.

Chapter Nine: Opinions and Eyeballs

At this point, I'm sure you've heard about the importance of both Google reviews and Yelp reviews. In fact, before making any significant decision, I'm sure you search for pertinent reviews. Maybe you even enjoy writing reviews yourself. And there is one type of review you haven't heard enough about, the LinkedIn recommendation. It's important to understand that recommendations on LinkedIn differ from endorsements for skills. While LinkedIn recommendations aren't as popular as Google reviews yet, they are valuable in establishing social proof and helping to influence potential clients in their decision of whether to do business with you and your company. The difference between recommendations and skills and endorsements is where skills and endorsements gave users a place to input certain skills; recommendations have nothing to do with endorsing skills.

I see people being endorsed for completely random skills they have no idea about, especially social media, marketing, and sales all the time. When it comes down to it, if you're a business owner, marketer or sales professional, getting business from LinkedIn has absolutely nothing to do with those skills and endorsements. No one's going to make their decision of whether to further engage with you, or whether to buy into your expertise based on the skills and endorsements you've received. However, recommendations are a different story.

If you visit most LinkedIn profiles, what you'll notice is most people do not have many, if any, LinkedIn recommendations. Now as a business owner, executive, marketer, or sales professional, this presents a lucrative and simple opportunity for you to distinguish yourself and your company. Speaking of LinkedIn recommendations, right here, right now, I'm going to give you six tips for instantly turning your LinkedIn recommendations into what I call marketing assets.

Number one, add requesting LinkedIn recommendations to your closing process. If you're like many business owners and sales professionals, you've probably caught on to the trend of asking clients for reviews. After you've wrapped a deal with a client, or during the process of working with them, include asking for a LinkedIn recommendation to your closing checklist. Whenever you close a deal, whenever you make a sale, or you sign on a new client, whenever you onboard someone, (and I'm sure you have a checklist and a process in place) add asking for a LinkedIn recommendation to that process. It doesn't matter your industry, it doesn't matter what audience you're selling to, whether you're in B2B, B2C, or whatever the case may be, you can apply this strategy to any business and any industry. And just keep in mind the goal is the more recommendations, the better. When you add this to a regular function of doing business, your profile will instantly jump out at people when they see you have a ton of LinkedIn recommendations.

If you don't have a checklist already for your closing process, I highly recommend you write one. I had a client suggest that to me, and I have found it's a simple thing to do. You can make it a regular practice to write your checklist and then apply it to different processes that you may not be too familiar with yet, like LinkedIn. It makes all the difference in the world to have a process in place and to use a checklist.

Tip number two is to tailor your recommendation to specific outcomes instead of character traits. Your best recommendation should reflect your company's unique selling proposition (USP) and unique value proposition. While there is nothing wrong with parts of a recommendation praising your personal character, especially when the recommendation is housed on your personal profile, you want to make sure the bulk of your recommendations are focused on results and outcomes. Doing so ensures congruence in your marketing message and helps your LinkedIn recommendations to become a true extension of your marketing mission. Strive to receive outcome-focused recommendations. I have noted so many recommendations on LinkedIn and on other social networks, that just talk about personal character and integrity. And while that's great, that isn't the feedback that's going to call someone to action, that will help them move forward in the process. If people talk about your expertise and character traits, absolutely embrace that. However, think about results and desired outcomes, because that's exactly what your audience is thinking about. It's just like we discussed in earlier pages. Remember that pivotal question: *What would your audience do?*

You should have a process and a marketing machine in place, and maybe you're in the process of building that. I'm someone who can certainly help you, because I help clients build marketing machines every day. So, if you don't have one you consistently use, reach out. But also recognize that we're always refining, we're always growing our marketing machines. LinkedIn recommendations should be an extension of your marketing machine and the marketing mission you use in your company. This third-party validation remains one of the most effective ways to reinforce your company's mission message. It also reinforces your social proof. Because it's one thing for you to say something great, but again, it's another thing for a third party to say something positive about you. Crazy how that works.

Tip number three is to recommend others. When you recommend others on LinkedIn not only will you gain that reciprocity, but you will also expose yourself to free advertising. For example, if you were to write a recommendation for me on LinkedIn, (which you're more than welcome to do, by the way), people viewing my LinkedIn profile would see your picture and your LinkedIn headline on my LinkedIn profile along with your recommendation. When they scroll through my recommendation section, it essentially means free ad space for you. This is such a simple way to drive extra traffic to your profile, your website, your marketing funnel, and at the end of the day, to your client lists.

And here's a bonus tip for you, a really tactical action, as of this writing. Your recommendations with the longest length will move to the top of your recommendations page. So, if you wrote me a recommendation that was the longest one on my page, you would appear at the top of my recommendation section, and everyone would see your profile picture, your headline and the recommendation you wrote. Powerful stuff as you can see, right?

Tip number four: Offer pre-written recommendations. This way, if your clients are busy people, which they likely are, they'll often agree to write you a recommendation, and then they'll forget to follow through. Tell me if that sounds familiar. Instead of taking it personally, all you need to do is provide them with the pre-written recommendation, a recommendation that is outlined and written from their point of view. When you send it to them, make it clear that they're free to make any changes or suggestions. Most of the time, what will happen is you'll just get an approval back, and you'll now have collected a personalized recommendation straight from them branded with their business name that you can use on your LinkedIn profile.

You can take this concept and use it with recommendations on other given steps in your other templates. You'll save them time; clients will be happy, you'll be happy. Everybody wins.

Tip number five: Connect with potential prospects on LinkedIn as part of your relationship building process. In prospecting, whether it's online or offline, I encourage you to ask potential prospects to connect with you on LinkedIn. One benefit of doing so will be that you will specifically use your LinkedIn profile as a marketing asset, especially when you have plenty of recommendations from clients. Your prospects can talk about the exact desired outcomes your current prospects are seeking. You can take this a step further when you apply some of the strategies from earlier in this book and beef up your profile to establish yourself as the authority figure in your space. Chances are your competitors have few, if any, LinkedIn recommendations, so you'll be able to use the recommendations you have as another way to set yourself apart. Doing so will be even more beneficial, especially if you follow the second step, and make sure the recommendations you receive are based upon specific outcomes. I cannot emphasize that point enough.

Tip number six: Repurpose your recommendations into LinkedIn posts. This is just like the content marketing that we talked about a little earlier, and here's another strategy you can apply. When a client recommends you on LinkedIn, they've shown you their openness to share the positive experience they had with you and to receive further exposure from their LinkedIn network, likely filled with potential leads who are similar to that client—and that's exactly what you're looking for. So, go ahead and take your client's recommendation and repurpose it into a LinkedIn post that you will then post to your LinkedIn newsfeed.

Find a photo of your client, preferably one where the two of you are together, and post that photo along with a snippet of the recommendation they wrote for you or that you wrote on their behalf and they approved. In the copy, which is the text above that photo, make sure to tag the client using the keywords followed by their name. This will automatically help LinkedIn to tag that client. What'll happen then is that members of your client's LinkedIn network will automatically be able to see and engage with the post. Now, these will all be members of your client's network. And the immediate members, members they have a close affinity with, will see that post, especially if your client sees it and comments on it, which they most likely will.

You now have six tips for growing your business through LinkedIn recommendations, a highly underutilized asset that you can absolutely take advantage of. It can feel like it's an ego contest sometimes, so just make sure you don't put too much emphasis on endorsements. Realize endorsements on LinkedIn, at this point, are overrated. Recommendations are the name of the game, now and when you apply these six strategies, they will reward you with the best results. This is a far better plan than receiving or seeking endorsements from everybody and anybody. Most of the time, when people endorse people, they don't even know if that person is viable for the skill. But that's an entirely different conversation we won't get into here in this book.

Next, let's talk about client networks. It's important to use systems that generate social proof, and it's important to leverage your clients' networks as well. Your targets should be people you've already done business with. You can scroll their profiles and gain access to everyone who's in their network. You'll not only see shared connections, but you'll also see everybody inside their LinkedIn network. So, if you have an ideal prospect, and you notice someone in your client's network who matches that description, let's say your client has hundreds of connections, mine through and make a list of potential prospects in that client's network. Have an assistant do this for you to save time. When you have that relationship with your client you can say, "Hey, I was just wondering, out of all these people, who do you feel comfortable introducing me to?"

There are a lot of great ways to ask. You can ask in a text, but better yet, talk to them in person or on the phone. However, when you communicate, just say, "You know, we've had such a great experience, and you received X, Y, Z results. I was looking to help out more people you know. So, out of all these people who you're connected to on LinkedIn, who would you be comfortable introducing me to?" When you ask them that question, I almost guarantee you that you will be able to receive a warm introduction.

A really good way to reach out, especially if that person is active on LinkedIn, is through the Messenger app, and the Messenger app is the chat box built into LinkedIn. Start a thread with the three of you in Messenger. Try saying, "Hi, this is (your name.) I thought the two of you should connect since you are blank and might be looking for blank." That's a simple way to start the conversation, and begin that process. I also encourage you to ask both parties if they have any interest in that introduction before making the thread. If one party isn't interested, you can prevent potential awkwardness this way and make the introduction at a different time. Now, you have the opportunity for a warm introduction. See how it's so much more powerful than trying to cold message, cold call or send a cold email?

Those are the lowest hanging fruit you want to make sure you're taking advantage of when it comes down to your clients' networks. And if you're doing that, and you're posting content that your clients are involved with and engaging in their networks, you are going to see more of yourself in there as well. You can also give your clients a heads up that you will be posting content and see if they'll engage. You can even syndicate it if your clients want to post as well. Maybe you have an agreement or a private group where whenever you post something to that group that everyone in that group agrees to engage with that piece of content. Then more people see it. This is yet another trick you can use to get in front of people's networks—people you already know—this is a powerful tool, too.

Let's talk a little bit about influencer marketing on LinkedIn. Who are the "influencers" when it comes to LinkedIn? I want you to think about influencers as being leaders within groups, leaders within subcultures, local groups and local communities. These are people who carry the clout of more than one. We can assume an HR director could very well be an influencer, because they have a big say in the company in controlling the employee benefits, for example. Other influencers might include board members of local chambers of commerce or associations. Identify the kind of influencers you're looking for; when you do this, it helps your clients as well, because then they can identify exactly the types of influencers they're looking for and how best to reach them. Once you've identified these influencers, you could build a targeted list and implement marketing specifically tailored to these influencers. When you build relationships with these influencers, they'll influence the communities that they're a part of to build relationships with you. Influencer marketing is another sustainable way of consistently connecting and networking on LinkedIn.

You want to make sure that if you don't know an influencer, you're not pitching them right off the bat. We'll talk about that in later sections of the book. Most influencers have a strong affinity for the group they're influencing and a part of, especially if they're volunteering, or in a community like the Chamber of Commerce. So, if you mention this fact in your connection request, for that very reason, many of them will be open to connecting with you and learning more about how you can further benefit each other.

You definitely want to identify influencers; you want to have conversations with them, to build influence in their networks. You can see when someone's posted on LinkedIn if they're getting massive engagement, or if they're being featured in the news. You can also find bloggers and, depending on your industry; you can learn which groups of people are relevant people in the media and on LinkedIn. When you become a part of these groups, they are a great place to show yourself in your best light. Especially when you've improved your profile and content, because that primes you to get that publicity and continued exposure as well.

When working with clients, I show them how to customize specific plans and follow through on their implementations, so they're able to make the most out of an influencer marketing network.

Are you really starting to grasp the idea of how powerful LinkedIn marketing can be for you no matter your industry, and how you can utilize it to make the most of your opportunities on LinkedIn? This is the new and exciting way of using LinkedIn to generate leads, receive referrals, and attract more high-end clients. If you're ready to accelerate your learning curve and start seeing results as rapidly as possible, visit Linkedleads.Us/Consultation to learn more about applying to work with me.

Chapter Ten: Powerful Partnerships

In business and on LinkedIn, everyone's always looking for a way to get their foot in the door and set that initial appointment to overcome the hurdle of being a stranger and that person who's coming in cold. We all agree if we've been in business, sales or marketing, for any length of time that the best way to get in front of someone is through a referral. People love doing business with people they know they can trust, and that's why everybody wants referrals. Not many people are going about it the right way, though.

You've got to be like Waldo when it comes to referrals. I'm sure you've read *Where's Waldo*? You know, the book with the weird guy, and he's got the shirt with the stripes on it. He's in those big pictures and blended into the background, and you have to find him. This analogy refers to the fact that a lot of people are completely unoriginal when building what I call powerful partnerships. That word "power," I want to personify that in a partnership, and that means a couple of different things. That means if there's business being exchanged, both people must be up to par. There's plenty of value being exchanged for that end user, as well. That's why

I use the word "power" instead of simply saying "referral partners," as so many people do.

Back to the analogy. When it comes to asking for referrals, a lot of business owners still take on the old-school approach of having their hand out, staring someone in the face, expecting them to pass business and not wanting to give anything in return. I may be exaggerating. I'm sure there's some value being exchanged, or if you asked one of the partners, they would say, "It's the relationship." That's how they are defining the value. While that has worked in the past, if you're looking to scale, you need more of those referrals and power partnerships. There's a new way to do it, and that is what we will go over in this chapter.

When it comes to power partnerships, the first thing you must consider and be completely aware of is what you want to look for in building these power partnerships. This applies, by the way, to every industry. It's a process that a lot of people still butcher, especially loan officers. There are a lot of loan officers running around chasing realtors, when the reality is that most realtors aren't even doing any business or aren't closing a substantial amount of business. You might be thinking your business is different or your model is different. But you can benefit from power partnerships in just about every industry. Whether you're digital or whether you're brick and mortar, there are power partners you can use to your advantage. The definition of a power partner is "someone who's doing business with people that you'd like to be doing business with and who can consistently refer new business to you."

Quality is super, super important. Here's the number-one thing when it comes to quality, the key question you must ask yourself: *Is that person solid?* Ethics is one of those terms that we're not going to get into here, but despite that, you still need to know if the person is someone who delivers value. Is that person reputable and trustworthy to a certain base of people? If the answer is yes, that's a very good sign. If the answer is no, you should probably not consider them to be a potential power partner for you.

Number two: Is that person doing a substantial amount of business already? If that person is not doing a substantial amount of business, there's got to be a different value proposition to substitute, and oftentimes, that's hard to identify, even though it's possible at times. You want people who have been in the business, but just know that experience can be a little bit misleading, as well. Experience is a loose word, because someone could be in business for 19 years and have no database. They would not have potential leads to throw your way. Or, vice versa, someone could be in the business for 16 months and have a ton of connections to pass to you.

Those are the three main things to look for at the beginning of a power partnership: credibility, value and experience. It starts off that relationship with the right level of rapport. Think of commonalities. For example, I have a client who's a U.S. Marine, so anyone he encounters on LinkedIn who's a potential power partner who's a Marine, of course, they're going to have that instant bond. Always also consider those intangibles, too, things that you do outside of business that allow you to relate to other people. This could be a good way to prospect potential power partners. Be willing to think outside the box to discover opportunities. Just because no one's doing what you conjure up doesn't mean you shouldn't do it. If all your competitors are chasing one vertical for referrals, e.g., loan officers and real estate agents, you could capitalize on groups that are much less sought after such as financial advisors, estate planners or even certain groups of investors that almost no other loan officer is seeking. So, don't dismiss or shy away from power partnerships that could pay off big for you.

When you go through the power partnership vetting process, you want to ask the same questions every single time to screen the quality of that connection and how legitimate that person is. Let's say you meet a power partner, a potential referral partner on LinkedIn and you set up that conversation. Usually, it's going to be over the phone. Sometimes you'll even have a meeting in person. Now, be critical with who you meet in person, because the time it takes to get to a certain location and back is an opportunity cost in and of itself. Only keep the high-priority meetings as in-person connections. Every other connection can be made over the phone, via direct message, video conference or chat, if that's your cup of tea. If you're doing business locally, you'll likely meet your new contact in-person.

These are some of the questions you will want to ask them, and you can also learn a lot from their LinkedIn profile. You can see experience, social proof, read if they have recommendations. You can determine how long they've been in their current position. Your screening questions, though, while they will be based on all those things, will also give you more information that is not as obvious, like the types of people they've partnered with in the past, what they'd be looking for in a referral partnership, etc. Your job is to see what kind of ideas they have, how open-minded they are. Oftentimes, the most skeptical people are going to be the ones you want referral business from. If someone has trustworthy clients, they may be guarding those clients, and with good reason, too, because there's a lot of scammers and fraudsters out there. You may meet these more uptight people especially if you take the old-school approach of after meeting someone recently that you just expect them to pass along their book of business. When you do this, and stick your hand out so prematurely, your odds of success are drastically decreased.

What's the approach to take instead on a site like LinkedIn? If you meet someone cold, you'll make that appointment, screen them and learn if they seem like a legitimate opportunity for a power partnership. Maybe they seem interested in networking and connecting, but some people, if they just have no interest, they have no interest. Move on. Some people are very closed off and stingy in that regard. Don't waste any more time. But don't sweat that lost contact that's not right for you anyway. In the next chapter, I'll talk about how on LinkedIn, you can find thousands, if not tens of thousands, of potential referral partners. You will want to read ahead to discover how the sea never dries up.

The new way of approaching these power partners is through using something called information marketing. Information marketing means applying education-based marketing to their databases. This means they take material, whether a webinar, PDF, in-person events, a free book, or whatever it happens to be and they give it away for free to their client base or their prospective client base, and they use that to reciprocate an exchange: for the opportunity to get in front of that client base. For example, if you're a loan officer and you're working with a financial planner, if you can provide something of value to that audience, they'll be much more likely to expose you to their connections. You can tell them you don't need a direct referral, necessarily. It'd be nice, and it's going to happen once in a while, so when it does— leverage it. But I am referring to an opportunity to get in front of that audience. It's important to remember what that would look like. Most people who have successful marketing and sales systems have some sort of database. You want the opportunity to mine and tap into their database without being spammy. The best way to do that is through the education-based marketing approach. Just ask for permission. "Hey, can I provide this free guide to your database?"

Better yet, you want to collect some leads from their database. To enable lead collection, set up something called a landing page. In case you're unaware, this is just a page someone can go to on any site—where they land. Usually, the simpler the page, the better. A lot of business owners make the mistake of just focusing on driving traffic, (which is the lingo word for visitors.) When we go to a website, it's usually just so overwhelming. It's a much more effective approach to just drive people to a simple page with a nice, big headline. This is also an opportunity for them to enter their information, usually their name and email address, and oftentimes, their phone number, especially if you're in a high-trust industry. If you're sending out something like a physical book, then you have justification to collect their mailing address, too. If you're doing any sort of direct mail or any similar marketing, you can gather their information as well.

You want the database to visit a landing page if possible, and for the visitor to enter their information on the landing page in exchange for something free of value. Whether, again, that's a webinar, PDF, book, etc. That's completely up to you. The rule of thumb, though, is to remember this is education-based marketing. This is not just education. You're not a school teacher sitting there in the schoolhouse just giving stuff away. You've got to make a living, as well. You want to give them enough information of value to where it's not a complete sales pitch. At the same time, you want to make it very, very clear that you're the go-to guy or gal for them to receive more, to have their problem solved. I work with clients on different kinds of presentations, and I've made the mistake of trying to educate without the educational marketing piece. So, structure your information in a certain way using psychology and marketing. Educational pieces inspire people to raise their hands and say they're ready to buy or ready for your consultation. That's a pretty big deal.

It's important to have their permission to approach that database. Better yet, if you're doing business locally, you can host an event that's in-person, or you can even do a webinar. The great thing about webinars is people don't necessarily have to make the commitment to show up and be there. These days, it's a big commitment to show up and to schedule a date that requires you to be somewhere. Instead, you'll still be able to collect that information. You're still able to provide value, and you can even use a video that's pre-recorded, so it fits in your schedule.

Let's recap. The information marketing approach to gain referrals works like this. You're going to ask for permission to provide education-based marketing to the database. In doing that, at the very minimum, you want a way to collect people from their database and incorporate them into your marketing system. You'll often see a percentage of people in that database who will be ready; they'll be willing, they'll be hot. Then, you'll see a percentage who are warm or just warming up to your idea. Finally, you'll have a percentage who just aren't in the market. In this way, you will gain maximum exposure, and you'll still get the hot ones.

If you used the old approach, leading with your hand out, you maybe would get a lead once in a while, versus if you consistently deliver educational-based material, then you have that solid opportunity to get in front of their database. At the end of the day, you're helping that referral partner out, too, because they're constantly looking for ways to provide value. Most businesses thrive on repeat business. So, you're educating for free, giving value, and providing your referral partner with a new angle that he can then share to give value to his database. Numbers do talk. If you're able to establish an affiliate or a referral program where someone gets a kickback, or you have that sort of relationship, all the better for you. That'll get the wheels turning even faster, especially if you're a digital business. Yes, there are compliance concerns that you need to be aware of, and I am not going to get into those in this book. That said, you need to know the rules. Referral programs are fairly easy to establish, and there's a lot of different software to help you track and monitor your data.

In a nutshell, power partnerships offer a new dynamic to leverage in your business. In the next chapter, we'll talk about ways to find your ideal prospects and power partners. I'll tell you about the approach that works. When I work with clients, this is what I teach. This is what I help them to implement, everything from creating content-based marketing to reaching out to those powers partners, to sealing the deal and getting in front of databases, to then helping them to follow-up so they can turn their interactions directly into new business. To learn more about applying to work with me, visit Linkedleads.us/Consultation.

Chapter Eleven: Locating Ideal Prospects

This next chapter includes my idea of what I consider to be the good stuff. We're going to talk about how to find your ideal prospects. At the beginning of this book, we talked about how so many businesses are still buying leads. They're scratching their head about where they can get leads, and my definition of a lead doesn't necessarily include someone who's a prospect. The prospect is someone who's either qualified to buy or has an interest in a product or service.

That said, let's talk about searches on LinkedIn. LinkedIn has one of the most capable search engines on the planet. You know, it's funny. We all think about search engines like Google, and some of us even use Bing and Yahoo. When it comes down to locating your ideal prospects on LinkedIn, you want to do a number of different things. Number one is you want to segment and see all the filters that are out there. As I'm writing this, I'm looking at LinkedIn.com to give you the search, so I can better describe it to you and so you won't miss any of the filters.

Let's say I search for the term "real estate." I'm going to see people who are connected with me first, people who have that keyword in their profiles. I've got two different filters on the LinkedIn search, and this is part of the reason it's so powerful and appealing. Number one, I can filter by my first connections, so if I want to see people, I'm already connected with who meet that criteria, I can go in and search that way. If you wanted to see people who are your second connections, who you share at least one mutual connection with, you could filter by second connections, as well, and you can filter by third-plus connections, as well.

You've got location, too. Any location you can name. Cities, towns, states, countries. You can also look for current companies. If you want to target potential leads in certain companies, or better yet, influencers within companies, then you have a chance to look at companies. There are also ways to filter by companies where people were formerly employed at, as well as by industry. If you can think of an industry, it's there on LinkedIn. Other filters include profile language and nonprofit interests. You can also see if someone shares a common university with you, common education, or common language. The search spans from finding universities all the way up to figuring out if someone went to high school with you. You can find all these filters in the right-side under the search features.

You can also search by job post. If you're prospecting a company and you want to find their level of activity or who they're hiring for, you can do what one of my connections who's a contractor did. It's a brilliant strategy. He checks out which companies are posting. Then he reaches out to the decision-maker who posted that job and makes them an offer. That's one way to do it. If you provide outsourced services, it's called a tripwire, which is a sign that contact is in the market for that product or service, and so you can directly reach the decision-makers.

You can also search by post, and find posts on LinkedIn that contain the keyword you're searching for in the LinkedIn feed. If a prospect is in the market for any product or service and you see which articles are getting the most engagement, you'll first be able to see which posts were posted by your first connections. You can also find company pages and groups as well. In the next few pages, we'll talk more about LinkedIn groups.

These are all filters which can be used through the basic LinkedIn search. It's a powerful search. I highly encourage you to play around with it. Not everyone is ready for what I'll cover next, the Sales Navigator. I get asked about the

Sales Navigator a lot, and many people have been quite frustrated with it, because they've invested in a premium account, and they haven't seen their results improve on LinkedIn. It's kind of like wanting to eat just the cherry on the top of an ice cream sundae. You're going to enjoy the sundae, and you've got the cherry on top. The same thing goes with LinkedIn Sales Navigator. That cherry on top is the premium account on LinkedIn. The most powerful thing about it are the searches, segmentation, and the various lists. Unless you have your strategy and marketing down, your profile is refined, and you know how you're going to reach out to people, that Sales Navigator is just a cherry on top. There are different premium features for LinkedIn as well. There's also the recruiter feature, which is essentially, a tool for searching and a CRM (customer relationship management) software for recruiters.

Then, you also have the classic premium account. If you're in business, marketing, or sales, I highly encourage you to use Sales Navigator. It's a much more powerful search, and you have a built-in CRM software. In the future, it'll probably integrate well with many other CRMs. But right now, it integrates with a couple of the top CRMs out there.

The Sales Navigator has a few more different filters and has two of the biggest advantages. Number one, if you're in B2B and you're hustling for enterprise-type accounts, you can find the exact decision-maker, much like you can through the regular search, but the bonus is you can save them as a lead, and you'll get a customized news feed of their activity and posts. The Sales Navigator will give you a tailored LinkedIn newsfeed that will show you when that person posts. They'll be easier to follow and build a relationship with when it comes down to prospecting. The next advantage is the advanced search filters. LinkedIn's regular search features are currently limited to conducting a certain number of searches per month. Once you go over it, LinkedIn will require you to upgrade. With Sales Navigator, you'll have unlimited searches. You'll be able to segment lists with specific criteria, using parameters like zip codes and titles. Far more accurate search results will come from the Sales Navigator search.

Another awesome benefit is that you'll be able to save different lists. When it comes to marketing, we talk about segmentation a lot, and segmenting customized messages to specific audiences can be critical. You'll be able to specifically segment by certain trends, geography, demography, trends inside companies, company sizes; you can create narrow, targeted lists. And you can go as wide or narrow as you please. That's the story behind segmentation. Again, don't be afraid to think outside the box when it comes to segmentation. Just because everyone in your market is targeting a certain type of prospect, you want to still go for your ideal prospects, even if your prospects don't match theirs. You want to prospect people who are qualified to do business with you. That's the chief goal. At the same time, be willing to prospect, especially for referral relationships, maybe think of those contacts no one else has talked to yet, that no one else has prospected yet.

Get familiar with these searches. They're constantly getting updated. You'll find thousands of potential leads to contact and connect with on LinkedIn. The great thing about LinkedIn and targeting and segmentation is most people don't lie on LinkedIn. People can lie and say whatever they want on other social media channels like Facebook. With LinkedIn, it's straightforward. It's official. You'll gather accurate data and build entire lists of prospects. Once you get your segmentation down, you'll learn how to start building those relationships that could potentially lead to new opportunities for you. We'll cover all that in the next chapter.

Precise segmentation and using LinkedIn groups to prospect can often be challenging. I show clients how to succeed in this endeavor and how to hone in on my digital programs when they come work with me. To learn more about applying to work specifically with me, please visit Linkedleads.Us/Consultation.

Chapter Twelve: Trojan Horse Prospecting

Do you remember the story of the Trojan horse? In case you're not familiar with the story, it's about a battle in ancient Greece between the Trojans and the defenders of a city who were not Trojans. Instead of launching an all-out attack, the Trojans knew they would be outmatched and decided on a subtle approach.

According to the story, they built a giant wooden horse and rolled it to the enemy gates as a gift and sign of their surrender. The delighted enemy brought the horse past the gates and began a festive celebration. Little did they know the Trojan soldiers were hiding inside the horse and were waiting to attack. During the celebration, the Trojan soldiers scurried out of the giant wooden horse and easily defeated their enemies.

Your best approach to pitching on LinkedIn is to model the approach of the Trojan horse. Meaning, you'll be more effective without directly pitching especially on the first message. Yet so many salespeople and business owners still think it's a smart move to pitch at the first touch point. When you do this, you take the high chance of alienating what could be a potential client and almost urge them to make the immediate decision of never wanting to do business with you. That risk isn't worth it, no matter how good your pitch is or even if you think you have the perfect pitch template.

When you identify a potential prospect on LinkedIn and want to move them through your sales process, your best bet is to build value and familiarity first. The way to do this is to connect with the potential prospect through a customized connection request. When you write it, you will show potential prospects why you wanted to connect and that you took the time to read their profiles before requesting to connect.

This is human psychology at work. We tend to do things more confidently when we see justification, no matter what that justification might be. In this case, you want to have a reason for connecting, whether that's the point that you admire their company or you're looking to meet like-minded people. Breaking it down to such a simple approach will often get your connection request accepted.

In the next chapter, we'll talk about ways to incorporate customized connection requests into your marketing funnel.

For now, though, just think about reasons you could justify a potential connection. Also, word of warning, your profile should not look like you're about to sell stuff. Some people make their LinkedIn profile a bit too extreme. So, whoever skims it, will note it's a complete sales pitch. Then they wind up losing the potential relationship.

The way I show clients how to market is to effectively implement enough of a business or sales angle, and then to balance that angle with a not too sales-y tone. When you format your profile like this, you will not scare off your prospects. When working with clients, I provide the specific templates to help them get more of their connection requests accepted. These templates are based on simple things like commonalities, and they use what I call best top funnel practices. Sometimes there might be offers that are included. Try it this way, and you'll be surprised by how many people accept your connection request.

A long time ago, when I first got my start on LinkedIn, so many people were so willing to accept my request; they were just open to connecting. If you want to increase your chances, make sure that you at least customize that aspect.

Take a sentence or two, customize it, and you'll be well on your way.

Once that potential prospect has accepted your connection request, you've made your first touch and can begin building a relationship. Your second touch, unless the prospect chooses to engage with you first, should not be a direct message.

Instead, you can visit the prospect's profile to see if they're posting content. Go under their posts, note if they're posting content and if they are, engage with one of their recent posts. You can like that post and leave a comment. To take it a step further, end that comment with a relevant question that will get your prospect engaging in a conversation.

Instead of acting as the usual spammer trying to pitch on that first message, you've engaged them in a conversation that's probably not directly related to your product or service. They'll get a notification on their phone that you've instigated conversation. They'll be likely to reply, especially if it seems neutral, which most of the time, it should be.

Now, you're on their radar. If your prospect hadn't taken a careful look at your profile, just out of sheer curiosity before you started this new thread of conversation, you can now be sure they will. That's why it's important to make the most out of your profile and maximize your LinkedIn presence if you haven't done so already. That's exactly why I have my mock profile formula that helps my clients.

Now that you've made a second touch and potentially even engaged your prospect in a public conversation, everyone on LinkedIn can see your conversation. It's not as intimate, not as direct, but people will be much more open to this sort of communication method rather than sending a direct message—even if you said the same thing on the thread as you would have said in a more personal message.

Make an easy third touch by endorsing them for at least three skills. People love being endorsed on LinkedIn, and the new design has made endorsements much rarer. You might ask, "Well, how are you going to endorse somebody if you're not sure that they're very good at what they do, or a particular skill set?" I just take their top skills, and it comes down to taking their word for it. I see all sorts of crazy endorsements on LinkedIn, they really don't have much value, but that person will get a notification that you've endorsed them. Odds are, they will then visit your profile to figure out why you have endorsed them.

It gives them a little compliment, a little nudge. It's a nice way to start a relationship, and now you've made three touches without directly messaging them—without pitching them or selling them anything. If your potential prospect regularly engages with content and you regularly check your LinkedIn feed, which helps when it comes to prospecting, you'll begin to see LinkedIn recognizing the affinity between the two of you. The old-school term for that is EdgeRank. If there's ongoing interaction, then guess what? Even in the regular feed, you'll see that person's post first.

You can even go one step beyond that. The next time you're engaging on their posts, engage in public but also use their post as an organic conversation starter through direct message. Now they've posted something; now you can directly message them and start asking questions based on their profile and posts until you get to the hook.

Stay with me in coming pages, and I'll talk about the hook and why that's so important to include in a direct message.

It's also a great idea to find a common interest that can connect the two of you before you go into any kind of sales pitch and end that first message with a question. People respond to questions, especially from strangers. It's funny; if you ask a person a question, then subconsciously they will respond in their mind, even if they don't directly answer you. As long as that question is innocent, it will help with subtle rapport building. I can expect to get a response a fair amount of the time. Using this approach will result in a lot more conversations and receptive prospects than pitching them on the first message.

So, how do you transition to the pitch? Well, just like in the story of the Trojan Horse, your pitch shouldn't feel like a pitch. Depending on what your product or service is, make sure to figure out a few soft-sell questions you can ask a potential prospect as you're moving through the conversation. Some of these questions might be, "Would you be open to learning more?" "Is (your offer) something you've ever thought about doing?" This is a lot subtler than just going for that appointment and being that intense salesperson. You want to raise their awareness and effortlessly ask for an appointment at the same time. Raise their awareness to realize the challenge you can help them solve and don't be afraid of pre-qualifying prospects before taking that next step.

What do I mean by pre-qualifying prospects? In the sales process, if your intention is eventually direct contact, don't be afraid to ask prospects a couple of questions and pre-qualify them before getting on the phone. In fact, I highly encourage you to do that before booking an appointment through LinkedIn. You want to make at least sure your prospect fits the minimum qualifications. Be willing and able to engage in LinkedIn Messenger and pre-qualify them there before even *suggesting* an appointment. This is especially true if that person is receptive in messaging you back. Don't be in a rush to just suddenly get them on the phone.

Much like the Trojan horse, your pitch should be well positioned to give you consistent results. However, as we know is true in sales and marketing situations, things don't always go as planned. When working with teams and individuals, I show them an approach to add value through following up on LinkedIn, which ensures more receptive and attentive prospects even if they're not ready to immediately move forward in the sales process.

Let's say you're consistently reaching out to someone, the money is in the follow-up, right? Because everyone's getting messages on LinkedIn so if you're at that point where you're messaging somebody, use multiple methods. Send them an email; message them multiple times; just keep the follow-up flowing. Another way to give value in follow-ups is to engage with whatever it is that they posted. Just ensure you get an answer as you're building through to reach that follow-up stage.

After the question, you will craft a hook. The hook question is a little bit unique, but the number one thing to remember is that your hook is all about marketing instead of selling.

In the next chapter, we'll talk about top funnel marketing approaches (which you will address after the hook) and how and why you can receive the highest results when you set up your funnel in a certain way. Not all funnel set-ups equate to the same results. Let's be clear on that.

Before we jump into funnels, let me share an effective pitch on LinkedIn. Number one, if you can use a store quote, email, and say their name, you will be leading with social proof. When I talk about marketing to the C-Suite, here's one approach I recommend. You can say something along these lines: "We worked with X (who happens to be similar to them or a director competitor)" or "We worked with other CEO's (or whatever their position is)," and then mention the major problem or pain point you can help them solve. I recommend that you take a minute and identify what that leading challenge is depending on the product or service you offer. Under that challenge, you can also identify three sub-challenges. Leading with challenges will help you hook their attention much more effectively than leading with features and benefits.

Notice what you're not doing with this approach. You're not going on and on about how great your company is. Because really, they don't care, and you're not directly selling or directly trying to set up an appointment. This is a simple LinkedIn message; you want to make sure that it's spaced out and use no more than two or three sentences. It will take no time to write and when you are done, send that bad boy out with no regrets.

You can do the same thing with your cold emails if you are inclined to use cold email. Just remember though, that part of it is a numbers game. The more emails you send, the more positive responses you'll be likely to receive. Also remember that a lot of your results can occur within the follow-up as well. Be willing and able to make five, six, seven touches. The goal is just to elicit a response. You want them to either say yes, they're open to learning more and then have that further conversation, where you can pre-qualify them and get them to the next step or figure out they're not open. If they say no, you can still recommend, or suggest something free for them. That way, you'll at least have them on a list. If not, you can keep that relationship on LinkedIn, and reach out again later. Set a reminder for yourself to reach out again in whatever amount of time is appropriate. (As long as your prospect is okay with it).

That's the permission-based approach when it comes to the Trojan horse prospecting style. As you're starting a conversation, you can also notice a tidbit on their profile; ask them a question they'll be likely to respond to and which will make them want to converse. Keep in mind, people's patience and attention spans are short so, you want to get to the point sooner rather than later.

You'll notice that unless you have that initial rapport, a lot of people just won't want to have a conversation. That's why

I'm all about marketing funnels instead of directly reaching out. You can still have a ton of success through direct communication, so don't be afraid to do it, especially if you're looking for appointments to fill your pipeline. There are certainly plenty of leads for you on LinkedIn. If you're ready to start booking even more appointments than you thought were possible through marketing on LinkedIn, I recommend visiting Linkedleads.Us/Consultation and learning more about applying to work with me.

Chapter Thirteen: Top Funnel Calls to Action

When I talk about a marketing funnel, I just want to be clear about the 97/3 rule. This is a rule I had to learn the hard way like many people. No matter what your product or service is, this rule probably applies to you. Out of all the people out there who are your potential leads, prospects, and who have the potential to do business with you, about three percent of them are ready to pull the trigger. They're hot; they're warmed up, they're going to pull the trigger, they're ready to take action now.

The other 97 percent are somewhere else in the funnel. Some people never make it down the funnel, some people get half way down, and the ones that do business with you end up coming out of the funnel. You'll always have most of your people toward the top of the funnel. By growing the top of the marketing funnel, you'll be able to funnel them down and turn them into more people who can invest in your products or services.

Now that we're clear on what top funnel is, also realize that you're marketing your offers, your presentations, and your messaging. It's important to differentiate as it pertains to different parts of the funnel. People who are in the top three percent, who are ready to buy, and who don't know you exist, are going to have a different marketing message sent to them. This group gets top funnel marketing.

A great way to do top funnel marketing is to use a dispatch board using the word "free." Give something of value away in exchange for getting people toward the top of your funnel. This is a great and low-pressure action to take, especially if you know you're getting potentially qualified prospects in the top of your marketing funnel. Oftentimes, what I'll recommend clients do, is come up with a free offer of a product or service they can give away for free, and that will be valuable to that potential prospect. In their connection requests, ask them if it's okay to give your gift away for free. If your prospect accepts the connection request, go ahead and give them that offer right away and then invite them to your follow-up. Depending on what your follow-up process is, you'll be able to collect that lead at least and put them inside your marketing funnel.

Giving away things for free is a great call to action, and putting your content on LinkedIn should include the aim to give gifts away for free whether that's a PDF, an e-book, guide, treasure map, webinar or whatever the case may be. You might be doing some in-person workshops; it doesn't matter what you give as long as it has value and it is free.

A lot of people, especially in the service- based industries, are still relying on offering a free consultation. You have to realize how much pressure that consultation puts on your prospect, because they know two things going into it. Number one, they know there is no such thing as free. They know there has to be a catch, or at least that's what they're thinking. Number two, it's a lot of pressure on them, because they know there's gonna be an offer. If you're worth a nickel or a dime as a marketer, business person or salesperson, you best believe there is going to be one. No one wants to be sold to, and the consultation is a great, great call to action. It's a solid offer for more bottom funnel prospects, but if you're talking about the top funnel, which is going to be your broadest base where most of your leads are, then just realize that you should ditch that consultation. Move past it and get creative.

I'll give you an example. Let's say you're offering them a free guide with five tips to get whatever result. They go in, pick up the guide, and inside the guide, there will be a call to action for them to take the next step which is the consultation. That's really the top funnel, and the bottom funnel welled down for you in a very basic example.

When you conduct business in this way, it eases a lot of pressure. If your prospect has any interest at all, they'll pick up something for free, and then you can market to them. Now, you have their permission, not to mention the fact that you're going about it far more creatively than the competition, who are still offering a consultation. No, you're giving something of value up front, then taking them to the next step.

Regard your marketing and sales process as that step-by-step process. Step number one is to get them inside the funnel. The best way to do that is to give something away for free. Make sure when you do, that you have a way of collecting, keeping tabs and following up on that lead. Whether that's just saving their contact information, sending out a marketing piece, then following up with them manually on LinkedIn or whether that's sending them to a page to enter their contact information, just make sure you're following up. Make sure you have systems in place for follow up. This applies to email marketing, too, and briefly, I will just say people have given email a bad rap, but email marketing can work. If you condition your potential prospects the right way and provide enough value as well as structure your emails in a specific way, yes, they will work.

The mistake that I see a lot of business owners do with email marketing is they just try to pack information or calls to action. Most of the time, they send stuff no one cares about. I met an insurance guy, and he sent out information about cleaning supplies and the best cleaning supply practices to his email list. Let's be honest. We're in the age of Google, if someone wants to learn more about that stuff, they're going to go on Google. They're not going to wait on his newsletter and open it and get excited because he sent out that information, that perceived value.

Don't be afraid to have some personality in your marketing and in your calls to action, too. Using that personality, telling stories, that's what's going to compel people. Keep that in mind with your top funnels calls to action. Be consistent when you're putting out content and in your calls to action. Reinforcement is a major thing when it comes down to a call to action.

Get clear, and keep your message and your marketing pieces as simple as possible. Give them the exact URL; tell them what to do; tell them what they'll get when they engage with you. Make it super, super simple. Make sure when you have your landing page that it will collect their information, and that you have included the message stating you won't spam and you won't sell their name. People want to know that, because people and businesses have done it. Those are top funnel calls to action here. Follow these fundamentals, and you'll get a lot more leads, and you'll have over the long run, and even in the short run, a lot more interested people investing in your products or services. Speaking of calls to action, if you haven't done so yet, visit Linkedleads.Us/Quiz to take my free quiz and see how your profile stacks up against the competition.

Chapter Fourteen: The Time to Stop Ignoring LinkedIn Groups Is Now

If you're on LinkedIn, you're probably familiar with LinkedIn groups. In fact, there are hundreds, if not thousands of LinkedIn groups across multiple industries, countries, and communities scattered across LinkedIn. When browsing through the groups you're already a member of, you'll quickly see that most of them are ghost towns. In most LinkedIn groups, third parties often post on other people's behalf. The engagement on that content is usually slim to none, so you'll see a ton of people just posting articles, posting things that are supposed to give value, and almost no engagement. You could go through hundreds of LinkedIn groups right now at this very moment and discover that thousands of supposedly active members are in groups, but most groups will have almost zero engagement.

Of course, there are exceptions. However, it's rare to hear someone speaking enthusiastically and telling people about a LinkedIn group. But these groups can be a great place for prospecting and marketing, especially since we'll likely see a resurgence of activity inside LinkedIn groups in the near future.

For now, here are three tips for using LinkedIn groups to start generating leads. Tip number one, which I think is a huge bonus, is to prospect in the right groups. I see so many business owners and sales professionals, especially real estate agents and loan officers, joining groups that are only filled with their peers and competitors. While like can attract like, your prospecting and marketing activities in these groups will likely be ineffective and obsolete. By all means, join groups and engage with others in your field. It's good to be around like-minded people. It's good to be around top producers, but don't expect that by doing that you will produce any new business opportunities. Instead, become a member of the groups your ideal prospects and referral partners have joined. To find them, use the search function and then ask to join.

If for whatever reason, you aren't approved to join a LinkedIn group, you can see exactly who the group's admins are without being a member and then you can directly message that admin and start building a relationship with them as you dig into why you weren't approved and work toward getting approved. Even if you are quickly approved, it's still a solid idea to connect with and cultivate relationships with group admins, because they can be power partners for you, especially if they manage a group that's full of your ideal prospects and referral partners.

Here's tip number two: Locate the groups your prospects and referral partners have joined. If your potential prospect or referral partner is already a first-degree connection, meaning they've accepted your connection request or you've accepted theirs, what you can do is visit their profile and see which groups that person is a part of. Chances are if that person is a part of that group, other people who are like them are as well. Under interests, you'll be able to see all the groups that person is a part of. At this point, all you have to do is join the right groups using the strategy above, and you will be surrounded by hundreds, if not thousands, of your potential prospects and referral partners.

Tip number three: Engage with content instead of posting content. When it comes to marketing on LinkedIn, it's usually a smart idea to do what your competition isn't. We talked about zagging when everyone is zigging. In the best-case scenario, your competition, the competition which is at least making an effort to stay active on LinkedIn, is trying to come up with compelling content to post in LinkedIn groups that'll attract their ideal clients. They, or the third-party posters on their behalf, are posting to groups and receiving little to no engagement every time. You, however, are willing to do things in a new way. Instead of contemplating the perfect content to post, scroll through the group feed of your ideal prospects and referral partners and see who's posting content. If the person posting content looks like someone you'd like to establish a connection with, engage with their content. This type of engagement is so rare in most LinkedIn groups; you'll have a great chance of getting their attention.

Don't just engage by hitting like. What you want to do is post a comment to it in response, then end with an open-ended question. Make sure to mention the person by using the "at" (@) symbol and their name, so they receive a notification, which will usually go straight to their mobile phone. Now you've been a part of an interaction that rarely happens in a LinkedIn group. You've organically started a conversation with a potential prospect or referral partner instead of just sharing content and wishing for results. Taking full advantage of prospecting and marketing in LinkedIn groups is a huge component of prospecting and marketing on LinkedIn.

Another question that I get asked a lot is, "Should I start my own LinkedIn group?" Many people are on the fence about it, so I'll break it down and tell you my experience with starting groups. At the time of this writing, and again this is liable to change at some point, LinkedIn groups are professional. They have some benefits. The biggest con, though, is people just don't seem to get excited, and they tend to be more deserted, so if you want to really build a true audience and affinity, unless you're targeting very specific segments like HR professionals, and even if you are, you want to ensure your group has a twist because the people who will join your group will be in a million groups already. Let your group have a bit of personality. We talked about how being boring on LinkedIn will make you look like everybody else, so it's important to share your unique spark in the name of your group and in establishing your group brand.

Groups are a bit of a challenge. They're not easy to produce and get people excited about. Once they take off, they'll start to grow organically, and if you want to enhance this growth, you can funnel potential leads into your group. What I recommend you do if you're looking to start any sort of group, is to look at Facebook first. Right now, Facebook has a lot better features for generating group engagement, promoting the group, and notifying group members, so start there.

If I were you, I would keep the LinkedIn group on the back burner unless you have a specific group of people who you know the LinkedIn group would be perfect for. In most cases though, Facebook groups are the way to go, and in most cases, you don't need a group at all. Because someone has already put people together in a way that would be quite like the group you would assemble. It's just your job to market inside of that pre-existing group.

As far as marketing to LinkedIn groups, that's a definite yes! You'll find loads and loads of your ideal prospects in those groups. And if you'd like to be a part of my free Facebook group, the Disrupting LinkedIn group, you can visit http://bit.ly/2nkXPaC and request to join.

Chapter Fifteen: Company Pages and Advertising

Do you remember when all the fuss was about getting likes on Facebook? Even the smallest boutique could organically reach thousands of people through its content without having to pay for additional boosting or advertising. I first marketed a company page on Facebook in the fall of 2013, which meant I came onto the scene late and just before Facebook started severely restricting organic reach. The page was for a new colony for the fraternity at the university I attended. I remember being amazed at how our post could literally reach thousands of people and get so much engagement for free. Nine months later, I was in for a rude awakening when I started my fan page, got a couple of hundred likes, and barely reached 20 people on some posts. Times have changed.

The reason I'm sharing this with you is to tell you about the extraordinary opportunity to grow organic reach for a LinkedIn company page and to reach people who aren't followers of your company. If you haven't been paying much attention to your company page, which I know I haven't, you have been missing an opportunity to potentially reach thousands of people and generate leads regardless of your company's audience being B2B or B2C.

First things first, you need to create a company page on LinkedIn. This is a simple process which usually takes 10 minutes at most. LinkedIn will ask you certain questions about the number of employees, type of company, and description. Then you'll be set to make your company page live, and you can link it directly to your LinkedIn personal profile. The best part is, LinkedIn company pages still have so much organic appeal and aren't just a means of running ads on LinkedIn. We'll talk more about ads here in a second.

Once you have your page set up, you can use these three LinkedIn content marketing tips to increase engagement and generate leads from your company page, all without paying for additional ads. Number one, include a call to action. We talked about this a little bit earlier in the book. End that piece of content from your company page with a call to action that you want your leads and potential clients to take, whether that's a top funnel call to action or a different call to action. Your call to action needs to center on whatever you're giving away, and where your prospect can go to learn more. Define your call to action as a place your follower can go to learn more about your company and to receive something of value, as they also provide you with their contact information.

Number two, engage with images. Even with the new interface, the LinkedIn newsfeed can still be a pretty unexciting place. Most people spend considerably less time on their LinkedIn newsfeeds than on newsfeeds for Facebook and Instagram. So, here, you have an opportunity to draw attention to yourself by posting images, and the images that perform well on LinkedIn are those that contain people. Give some behind the scenes images on LinkedIn and post pictures of your employees, especially when they've been recognized for a milestone or achievement.

Another way to enhance engagement on your LinkedIn images is to make sure they are large enough to make people stop scrolling. Most users are on mobile, so large images will be much more likely to catch their attention. You can also include a simple call to action with your image such as inviting people to hit like if they can agree or relate to your post from your company page. The way LinkedIn's algorithm is set up, it'll put up your company's content, (for free by the way), in front of people who aren't following your company's page when someone in that person's network liked the post or engaged with it.

Here's the deal with mentions. Use the at (@) button to mention people when you are posting to your company's page. When a contact is mentioned in your company's post, you'll get further exposure to their network, especially when that person reciprocates engagement. However, there's a right way and a terrible way to use mentions. You don't want to come off as spammy by mentioning everyone you know in a company post that's completely unrelated to them. Mention people in relevant posts, such as posts congratulating a friend on a milestone. You can also mention your company page when posting from your personal page to add exposure.

Also, be willing to ask some of your business' current fans and clients to follow your company page on LinkedIn. They probably don't follow many company pages on LinkedIn, and by following will be able to see many of your posts organically. Having followers can also increase your credibility. If and when you decide to run LinkedIn ads, you will see if a connection is following a company's sponsored posts. Any time you see a company post in your newsfeed, you can see which of your friends are following that company.

Should you be advertising on LinkedIn? A few days ago, I saw an intriguing YouTube video: (http://bit.ly/2tnkeYa). The founder of Vungle, which is a startup, told the story of how he hacked LinkedIn ads and got directly into contact with CEOs and angel investors for as little as 16 cents per advertising campaign. You read that right: 16 cents. Of course, the rules of LinkedIn advertising have changed recently, and more so than ever before, LinkedIn wants more businesses advertising with them. This is because ad spend is one of the main ways the company generates new revenue.

LinkedIn ads and LinkedIn marketing were created to convince users to try LinkedIn ads, but these ads appear on Facebook. How crazy is that? It seems like when it comes down to Facebook, that everyone has tried to figure out advertising and is trying to use Facebook ads to grow. In fact, you may still be asking yourself if LinkedIn advertising is right for you. If you're a business owner or sales professional, you may find my answer somewhat surprising. Let's start with the facts.

LinkedIn's ad manager has come a long way and is the best we've ever seen. In the past, the only kinds of advertisements we saw on LinkedIn were sponsored banner ads on the sidebars. Today, even though banner ads still lurk on LinkedIn, we see many different ad shapes and sizes. Companies and individuals can pay to send Sponsored InMail, which is a cross between cold emails and direct mail. InMail automatically floats to the top of a user's inbox, and the user can choose to accept or ignore the messages. Then there are bulletin ads that run on top of pages in the LinkedIn newsfeed. Running these ads is like buying a bulletin board on LinkedIn to get your company noticed. LinkedIn also now offers sponsored/promoted posts, meaning companies can target and appear in users' newsfeeds as they're scrolling. These ads tend to be the most used on Facebook, but keep in mind that most LinkedIn users spend significantly less time scrolling through their LinkedIn feeds than Facebook users do. So, these ads might not be as worthwhile to post on LinkedIn.

You can also choose how you pay for the LinkedIn ad. You can select pay per click (PPC), or bid per thousand impressions. Another new feature of LinkedIn advertising is the addition of lead forms. Now, advertisers' potential prospects can fill out their contact information without having to leave LinkedIn. It looks like the golden age of LinkedIn advertising will be here soon, especially as users begin to become more active on the platform. LinkedIn just surpassed the 500 million user mark and shows no signs of slowing down since their recent acquisition by Microsoft.

With all the information you've just read, you may be ready to jump in and start advertising on LinkedIn, but should you? My advice: Proceed with caution. You see, most business owners, sales professionals, and marketers are far from experts when it comes to advertising. In fact, there are a few foundational misunderstandings which are holding them back. The first thing to consider before advertising on LinkedIn or any platform is: How will you be able to predict the audience's responses to your advertising message? At this point, LinkedIn is not the best place to test new marketing messages, and doing so can prove costly for small businesses and sales professionals. Also, consider the objective of the advertising campaign and temperature of the traffic. Will you be advertising to cold, warm, or hot traffic on LinkedIn? Sending a stellar message to the wrong traffic temperature will still result in an ineffective ad.

Before advertising on LinkedIn, also be aware of your marketing and sales funnels and where you intend to funnel traffic. If you think decision-makers will buy, and take immediate action because they saw a LinkedIn ad, well, you shouldn't be advertising on LinkedIn.

Who should be advertising on LinkedIn? If you already have a proven message and a proven audience along with a proven funnel and at least $500 a month to begin with that you can allocate into experimenting with LinkedIn ad campaigns, then you're probably well qualified to be advertising on LinkedIn. Also, understand that your cost per lead is still going to be higher on LinkedIn than it would be in most cases on Facebook and even Google PPC. The major advantage to LinkedIn ads is the precise targeting, especially as it applies to business owners and sales professionals who can earn substantial income when they acquire a new client. For most business owners and sales professionals, advertising on LinkedIn isn't the best option yet. However, expect that to change soon. If you are a skilled advertiser who already has effective ads and marketing funnels, it might be the perfect time to get in early and take advantage of the new opportunities LinkedIn advertising presents.

Also, keep in mind when you use the Sales Navigator search, and you're talking about segmentation and building audiences, that those searches use nearly the same segmentation features as the LinkedIn ads manager. You can run campaigns manually as well as through your messages, which tends to be a more effective approach. Again, there's no one-size-fits-all answer to this question. If you'd like more information, this is a strategy I teach clients. We originate campaigns, choose the best campaign, execute precise targeting, get results, and generate leads through different sorts of campaigns. That's LinkedIn advertising. Positively ever-changing. Expect more changes. Expect more and more opportunity. If you'd like my help with your advertising campaigns, visit Linkedleads.Us/Consultation to learn more about applying to work with me.

Chapter Sixteen: LinkedIn of the Future

I'd like to invite you to peek at the potential future of LinkedIn and marketing on LinkedIn.

Now before getting into it, let's make one thing clear. I do NOT work for LinkedIn and have no official connection to LinkedIn or any of its company policies in any way, shape, or form. I'm just a marketer who happens to have his eyes on the latest trends along with an advanced understanding of successful marketing on LinkedIn.

Without further ado, here are four future trends for you to keep an eye on when it comes to the future of LinkedIn:

1. Resurgence of Groups

If you're in any LinkedIn groups at all, you'll quickly see that most of them are ghost towns. What you'll find in most LinkedIn groups is that people, or often third parties are posting on behalf of people, sharing content. The engagement on that content is usually slim to none.

Just last week, a client asked me if I thought LinkedIn groups were dead.

I'll give you the same answer I gave her. While LinkedIn groups are certainly on the decline, they can still be great places to prospect and build relationships when you use the right strategies. Furthermore, I expect to see a resurgence of LinkedIn groups sooner rather than later.

LinkedIn has worked very hard to make groups more user-friendly, which I have seen firsthand from starting my own LinkedIn group. That group is still there, but I'm choosing not to actively build it for now and am instead building a Facebook group.

You may be thinking, *why is the supposed "#1 LinkedIn Expert" building a Facebook group instead of a LinkedIn group?*

Simple, I'm aware enough to see what works and use it to my advantage, and you should be, too. When, not if, LinkedIn groups begin experiencing a resurgence, I'll get to building the new LinkedIn group as a marketing asset.

Keep an eye out for LinkedIn groups to come back and be more popular than ever.

2. Video

Video is the clear trend in marketing right now. With attention spans as short as they are, videos can still get people's attention. As of this article, LinkedIn doesn't allow directly uploaded videos to the network. Instead, you're required to upload to YouTube first before sharing on LinkedIn.

Much like Facebook, that's a trend we'll probably see changing soon. LinkedIn has already gone above and beyond to become a content hosting platform with tools like Publisher and SlideShare so having a video platform sounds like a natural fit.

In fact, I anticipate LinkedIn going beyond that step and introducing its own version of live streaming.

How powerful would that be?

Let's say you've strategically built a network on LinkedIn full of potential prospects and referral partners. These people would get notified every time you posted a live video, which would be similar to how Facebook notifies your friends when you do Facebook Live.

Not only would live video on LinkedIn take content marketing to a whole new level, but it would also allow for companies and sales professionals to do live Q and A's for prospective clients and recruits as well as give a true "look behind the curtain" into real-time, day-to-day operations.

My imagination is already running wild with all the possibilities using live videos would have for marketing on LinkedIn.

3. Article Views

In the past, most of my article views on LinkedIn Publisher would come from people outside my first-degree network due to LinkedIn's algorithm and the type of audience I had cultivated.

More recently, most of my views have originated from my first-degree network. However, most views on my content outside of my articles still come from my second-degree network.

I welcome this change quite a bit. As someone using content marketing on LinkedIn, it's nice to get in front of my more immediate network when putting together specific content such as articles I've posted through Publisher.

The more someone reads your articles, the more affinity they develop for you as an expert and as someone they know, like, and trust.

4. Active Users

Most clients I work with tell me they've had a LinkedIn profile for years but aren't very active users. By now, I'm surprised if that has NOT been the case.

Especially since its acquisition by Microsoft, LinkedIn has been making a strong effort to re-engage many of its users and encourage them to become more active on the professional network.

Despite being somewhat confusing and user-unfriendly in the past, this new interface has made using LinkedIn simpler than ever. The mobile app has come a long way, which needed to happen since most people access LinkedIn via their phones or tablets.

There's no reason to expect the trend of users becoming more active on LinkedIn won't continue, especially if those users are business owners or sales professionals. And millennials, surprisingly enough, are the fastest growing demographic of LinkedIn users.

For LinkedIn to be successful, it will need a more active user base. A more active user base means advertising on LinkedIn will become more lucrative for small businesses and more users will appreciate the value of paying for Sales Navigator and Premium accounts.

In fact, there has never been a better time to start using LinkedIn more actively. The key is to implement the right strategies so you can enjoy a return on investment of the time and resources you've spent on the number-one social media business site in the world. To learn more about receiving my help in implementing the LinkedIn marketing strategies that will work best for you, visit Linkedleads.Us/Consultation to learn about applying to work with me.

About the Author

Yakov Savitskiy is a Nationally-Recognized LinkedIn Marketing Expert and the Author of *Disrupting LinkedIn: The Definitive Guide to Generating Leads, Receiving Referrals, and Attracting High-End Clients Through Marketing on LinkedIn.*

He has consulted with nationwide clients including CEOs, Best-Selling Authors, and Leaders of Seven-To-Nine-Figure Sales Organizations.

A sought-after speaker, Yakov has reached audiences of over 50,000 and delivered keynotes at The FIT Marketing Workshop, Albuquerque West Chamber of Commerce, and Infinity Business Networking Group in addition to other venues.

Yakov immigrated to the United States at just 18 months old and grew up in Atlanta, Georgia. Now a resident of Las Vegas, he believes freedom and financial independence lead to fulfillment.

Made in the USA
San Bernardino, CA
08 August 2017